Corporate Renaissance

"In the new thought we do not set goals. We do not plan. We take our steps without knowing exactly where they will lead us. We do have expectations but not specific ones. Life is not a complicated matter with which we have to wrestle and struggle. Life is more than a struggle to survive; it is one big adventure. Yes, every minute is an adventure. We see that every event—small or big, positive or negative—leads us forward."

"In the new thought there are no 'musts.' We do not do something because it is expected of us. We do what we want to do, what gives us joy, stimulation and meaning. Because the foundation of our actions is within us, our true resources can emerge."

"Within every human lies a creativity that—given the right milieu —has hardly any limitations. To set free these inner resources and to allow this creativity to blossom is now the great challenge. Here lies the true potential for growth."

"The human mind is progressing beyond the old perception of the meaning of business. The human mind is continually growing, stretching, raising human consciousness. So what is happening is that individuals are changing and business has not caught up. Individuals are already absorbing the new thought. They are not focused on surviving, but rather on living and, by continuous development, reaching their full potential."

CORPORATE
RENAISSANCE

ROLF ÖSTERBERG

CORPORATE RENAISSANCE

BUSINESS AS AN ADVENTURE IN HUMAN DEVELOPMENT

NATARAJ
PUBLISHING

Published by Nataraj Publishing
P.O. Box 2627
Mill Valley, CA 94942

FIRST PRINTING MAY, 1993

ISBN: 1-882591-12-7

Printed in the United States of America

10 9 8 7 6 5 4 3 2 1

EVERYONE IS ENTITLED TO A MEANINGFUL LIFE

(From the United Nations Declaration of Human Rights)

TO
KELLY, CHARIESE, CIRBY, PATRICE
and
LUCAS and MAX
The new generation . . .

CONTENTS

Introduction

During the 1960s and 1970s, I made my career in Swedish business. For about twenty years (until the middle of the 1980s) I worked as an organization and business executive and was strongly committed to what I was doing. I felt that I was participating in something important: the continuation of the development of the economy and welfare of my country through business activities. I was relatively conservative politically and had a firm, classically conservative opinion regarding the interplay between capital and labor.

The driving force of development, as I saw it, was economic growth, regardless of whether that was reflected in our paychecks, the profit and loss accounts of the corporations or the finances of the state. I recognized the necessity of fair distribution of this growing wealth, but I also attached great importance to the interests of the capital investors. Without risk capital, the economy could not grow.

By the end of the 1970s (I was then in my early forties) feelings of emptiness and meaninglessness started growing within me. I began having doubts as to whether my basic assumptions about business and economics were actually correct. That frightened me.

These doubts came to me most strongly during the labor negotiations in which I was then heavily involved. For many years

1

I was president and CEO—eventually chairman—of the Swedish Newspapers Association. In those capacities I was responsible for the nationwide collective bargaining of the newspaper and magazine publishing industry. Through most of the 1970s I was also part of the top management of the largest newspaper company of Scandinavia, the Dagens Nyheter Group (now the Marieberg Group) and was responsible for the in-house labor negotiations.

Inevitably, the final round of negotiations consisted of waiting. Because this often occurred during the evenings or early mornings, I developed the habit of walking around the block during the waiting periods. It was on these walks that I often felt a sense of uneasiness and discomfort. These feelings had nothing to do with the expected result of the negotiations, but with what we were actually doing. We were purchasing and selling human labor. We were regarding humans—their knowledge and skills, their time and a great portion of their lives—as a commodity. This viewpoint was not unique to the representatives of management; the union representatives looked at the matter in the same way. Even more striking, however, was that this view was not limited to the representatives of each side. The people who made up each side—labor and business—took the same approach.

The employees regarded themselves as a commodity and assigned their representatives the task of selling this commodity for the best possible terms. To them, the company was nothing but a tool—a tool to make the money needed for survival or to make a career, to reach position and power. This corresponded with the view of the employers, who wanted to acquire the commodity at terms best for them and who, in turn, regarded the employees as *their* tools—tools to realize their business and, for that matter, their personal goals.

We management representatives viewed our positions in the same way: we, too, were selling our skills, our time and large parts of our lives. We were tools for our employers, and we regarded our working places as tools for our goals.

"There must be something more to work and business," I said to myself during those hours. "This is nothing but pure mechanics. People are only tools, units of negotiations, cost factors. There is no real life in the whole enterprise."

I pushed the thoughts away; they scared me. If I followed these lines of thought, where would it end? Isn't growth what we are aiming for? Isn't growth in the interest of all? Isn't profitability what we are aiming at? Isn't that in the interest of all? Haven't I, as have most others, based all my existence on these goals? Could there be any driving force, any motivation, other than an improved material standard?

"Be careful, Rolf," a voice inside me warned. "You are thinking yourself out of the market! Consider your career, your position, your image, your finances. Protect yourself and what you have obtained!"

Later—in the middle of the 1980s—I left my position and most of what was connected with it. Symbolically enough, I was then president and CEO of a company that produced, distributed and exhibited illusions: AB Svensk Filmindustri, the largest film company in Scandinavia. I found myself in an unusually privileged situation: I was given breathing space and the opportunity for what I would like to call a long inhalation.

Yes, it was a privileged time, but also probably the most difficult period of my life. I'll try to explain why.

As a young man I had set goals for my life. I did not reflect too much about the deeper meaning of those goals or about my life's purpose. For me, as for most of my generation, my goals were the conscious or unconscious projections of what I felt were the expectations of the world around me. My thinking about my future had little to do with what I felt, deep within myself, I wanted to do with my life. For me, the main issue was to get a good job in the mainstream economy and to succeed, to show that I was somebody, to show that I, according to prevailing standards, was good enough. For me, as for so many in my generation, this meant to climb the societal ladder, to make a career.

Then I woke up. I saw that I had reached my goals relatively early in life. In fact, I had succeeded faster than most in my generation. Thereafter, I had occupied myself with an ongoing process of protecting what I had achieved and of finding out how to climb even further. Yes, I had succeeded. But did I feel any joy, any satisfaction for having reached and even surpassed my goals? Did I feel that I had used my resources, used myself, if you will, in a meaningful way?

No. I woke up with dissatisfaction. I woke up feeling empty and meaningless. I woke up discovering that, by strongly focusing on my career, on my goals, I had lost myself. I had become so absorbed by my professional role that I had lost my true identity. I had so strongly identified myself (and had been so strongly identified by the surrounding world) with what I had achieved, that neither I nor anyone else really had any idea of who I was.

Having left my position, having left what I and the surrounding world had identified as me, I found myself walking in a quagmire. I found myself without any firm ground under my feet, without any hold on my existence. I found myself losing weight. I found myself more restless than ever before. I found myself drinking too much. I eventually came to the understanding that I had to start what has turned out to be a long and arduous road to break the armor around the real me in order to rediscover my true identity.

My feelings of emptiness and meaninglessness were transformed into a blend of grief, anger and longing for something else. I felt grief similar to what we feel after losing a loved one.

I was mourning the loss of what I had believed in, the loss of what had been the basis of my life. Much of my anger was because I felt betrayed—by my upbringing, my school years, my university years, by all society. Everything I had been taught was wrong! Everything I had been induced to believe in was wrong!

Or, had I really been betrayed? Had I really been induced into those beliefs? Could I really blame my surroundings? Had I not, myself, been part of all that? If there were a betrayal, weren't I the one to blame? Had I not betrayed myself?

And, was it really wrong? Isn't what is "wrong" or "right" what we collectively believe is wrong and right? Aren't societies, our political systems, our educational systems, our economic systems, the ways in which we look upon and conduct business, what work really means to us and so on a result of our way of thinking, a direct consequence of our perception of life?

What if we are changing our thinking? What if our thinking in one direction has gone so far, become so extreme, that it in itself has created a platform for new thinking, a platform for a new step in human development?

Having collected myself, I dared to express my questioning. I dared to express my doubts as to whether what was once right really still was. I dared to express my longing for something else. I discovered that the questioning that had started growing within me was in no way unique to me. From many directions—some of them very unexpected, indeed—came the same signals of doubt, the same questioning and, not the least, the same longing.

I became more and more convinced that something great, something much greater than I had ever believed, is happening, and it is happening to all of us. We are indeed changing our beliefs. We are indeed changing our way of thinking. And the bridge taking us over from what I call the old thought to the new thought is our growing search for meaning. More and more of us find that the world that surrounds us does not correspond with our thoughts about meaning. The terrain (the systems in which we live) no longer corresponds with the map (our minds). The map is changing and the terrain must be adjusted accordingly.

I decided to write my thoughts. I decided to make use of my experience in a hectic, sometimes fun, but, above all, learning business career to ponder about the effect of these changes when it comes to the issues of work, business and the economy. My book was published in Sweden in the spring of 1990. I was amazed at its reception, at the interest and respect it caught in the media, at the discussions it caused. I was, above all, amazed—and very happily so—at the hundreds of spontaneous letters and phone calls from readers of all categories: workers, business leaders, artists, physicians, priests, psychologists, air force officers, union leaders, and not the least, all those young people from all parts of our society! Everyone wanted to express the same thing: "This is what I have been feeling for a long time now. Thank you for putting words to my feelings."

Since 1987 I have been married to an American, and have had the chance to live six months of the year in Sweden and six months in the U.S. This has given me the privileged opportunity to compare the two countries. My questions was, "Is this something specific to Sweden or Scandinavia, something emerging from our history? Or, is the same thing happening in other parts of the word? Is it happening in the U.S.? My conclusion—based, among other things, on the response to the lectures about my thoughts—is, Yes, the same thing, the same evolution, is taking place in the U.S. In the U.S. (as, for that matter, in any country where I have had the opportunity to express my thoughts, including Germany, Switzerland, Italy, Great Britain and New Zealand) I see the same questioning and the same doubts. And I sense the same longing.

All this encouraged me to translate the book into English and make the changes and extensions I saw appropriate for the U.S. audience. My friend Samuel Matthews helped me with the first editing. I was lucky to make contact with an agent, Sandra Martin, who connected me with my editor, Leslie Keenan, and with my publisher. So, here I am at the beginning of yet another adventure: my meeting with you, dear reader. And when it comes to meetings, I know they have something to teach us. I must admit that I am very curious about what this meeting will teach me.

Something more: When reading this book, please keep in mind that these are my thoughts. This is the point I have reached so far in my thinking. I am convinced that I am on the right track. But I am not out there to necessarily convince you. Please question my theses. The only thing I really want is to plant a seed in the ground and to see that seed start a process.

CHAPTER 1

Our Contract with Nature

*D*uring the last few years, I have been spending more and more time in close contact with nature in different parts of the world. For me, as for so many others, this closeness to nature has become a vital need, a precondition of life. Whether walking along a beach at the Pacific Ocean or sitting on a boulder in a Swedish forest, I get the same feelings from nature. It can be a *wemut* (melancholy), or an intense, undefinable longing. It can also be a righteous and sometimes raging anger over the way that we humans—"the masters of nature"—exploit, consume and devour our surroundings to achieve our shortsighted, selfish and materialistic purposes.

But, above all, the contact with nature gives me a strong feeling—yes, even clarity—that everything is interconnected. In nature it becomes obvious that each part of what we call creation is intimately related to and a part of every other part of creation. And, if we only gave ourselves some time to observe and listen, we could not avoid seeing that we humans are parts of that whole, living system that nature is displaying to us. We would see that, although nature is our servant, we are not its masters. We would see that what we do to nature we do to ourselves. We can learn much from nature about human relations and, with that, much

9

about work, business and economy, for these matters are essentially nothing but human relations.

Most of us enjoy being in nature and spending time there. It's true of people all over the world. I often wonder, How is it possible for leading industrial entrepreneurs, after a walk in the forest or a hike in the mountains, to go back to their offices and, for example, send forth enormous machines to clear-cut— slaughter—entire forests?

How is it possible, after a sailing tour in the beautiful waters that nature offers us, to negotiate an increase in the amount of pollution that can be put into those waters, for instance, to reduce by $25 to $150 the production costs of a $25,000 car?

How is it possible for a government chief to one day walk along a beloved seashore and exchange it the next for some small increase in new jobs, to negotiate away a piece of nature, a piece of us? Do the governments own nature? Do they own us?

What caused us to terminate our contract with nature? What created this distance—this abyss—between humans and nature? How have we come to regard nature as something detached from us, a somewhat picturesque feature of our existence we go out to view now and then much as when we go to a zoo to watch wild animals? Shall we finally confine ourselves to some scattered national parks as memories of the vastness that once surrounded us?

How meaningful is work that encourages this development? What kind of basic beliefs within our economic systems drive us to this?

I cannot shake these questions, and I will come back to them.

CHAPTER *2*

A Time of Transition

*W*e are living in a thrilling time. It is a time of unrest and upheaval; we are at the end of one developmental era and on our way into a new one. This change is not small. It is much more profound and revolutionary than we can imagine. It implies a revolution in our way of thinking, a revolution that turns upside down our learned, ingrained conceptions about human beings and about life. This change could be threatening to some, but it is wise for us all to take it seriously. It cannot be halted. It has its own natural developmental force. It is strong, and it is rapid. All aspects of our lives are affected.

Our old way of thinking is being replaced by a new one; an old thought is being superseded by a new thought. In this book I refer to them as the old thought and the new thought. The result of the process of trading old thoughts for new thoughts is a giving way; the predominant male (logical) aspects of our thinking are giving way to the female (emotional) aspects within us. It is important, though, to keep in mind that this is not a case in which the pendulum swings from one extreme to another. Rather, the pendulum swings from one extreme into balance; a union between our male and female aspects is emerging. Let me clarify with an example close to us all: money. In the old way of thinking we focused on results. Money, then—in the extreme manifestations of the old thinking—became the overall yardstick and consequently a goal and an end in itself. In the new way of thinking, we focus on process not results, but that does not mean that we erase the issue of money. Money now becomes a means to maintain the process and also—as will be explained later—the by-product of the process.

This shift of thinking affects all parts of our existence. To some extent, we have already seen it affect areas such as physics, medicine and psychology. For me it has become particularly tempting to ponder what this development will mean for business life— for work, for companies, and for our economic system—partly because it is within this sector that I have obtained most of my professional and life experience. It is also, however, because I am convinced that business, with its ability to respond quickly to change, is the sector that offers the largest potential to address and to move with the new thought. Business, therefore, could play an important role as a bridge between the old and the new thought and thus contribute to a less traumatic and reasonably smooth transition.

This is, in itself, a bit paradoxical. On the one hand, it is in business that we see the foremost examples of the old way of thinking; in business we most clearly see the extremely logical and material manifestations of the old thought. At the same time, however, I cannot see any other sector of our societies having a better ability to sense "what is in the air." Furthermore, I don't see any other sector with an equal ability, inclination and willingness to adjust and change. No other sector has the flexibility of the business sector.

To all appearances, the business life of the whole world is on its way into a deep crisis. Even though the outer manifestations of this crisis concern economies, I am not now referring to the current recession or that depression so many predict will occur in the near future.

I refer, instead, to an existential crisis over the purpose and meaning of work and business. Businesses that address this crisis and go through it will survive. Businesses that close their eyes to what is happening or perhaps resist change by growing more rigid and withdrawing will have little hope of survival.

Before going further into this, I must clarify what I mean by the old thought and the new thought. I address these issues in the following two chapters.

CHAPTER 3

The Old Thought

*T*he old thought has now reached its ultimate conclusion and has become extremely logical. It fragments the whole and allows individual parts to conceal the whole, blocking the larger perspectives. For instance, the old thought measures growth in economic terms and does not see that this growth, in a larger perspective, is a fallacy; this "growth" requires an ever-increasing rate of consumption of our total resources and is factually negative.

The old thought tries to cure symptoms instead of trying to find the root of the problem.

The old thought is linear. It extrapolates the future out of the past and starts from the maxim "bigger is better."

The old thought is quantitative; it has to measure and explain everything. What cannot be measured or explained is not accepted. With the old thought the intellect governs and emotions are suppressed. In fact, the old thought is afraid of emotions. It analyzes and calculates; it plans and makes up strategies. Typically, it sets goals and then walks directly toward them on straight and narrow routes, blind to what is happening on either side. (Education, for instance, is goal directed and preferably "leads to a profession.") The old thought leaves few opportunities to, as I put it, "catch the moment in its flight." It leaves little, if any, space for intuition. I have witnessed the destruction of many brilliant ideas as they were literally calculated to pieces.

The old thought evaluates and judges. It is intolerant. Perceptions and behaviors deviating from the general pattern are threatening and, thus, not acceptable.

Economic Growth Is All That Counts

The old thought is inherently materialistic. Success and progress are measured by the yardstick of money and possessions. The purpose of work is to make money. The purpose of business is to make a profit, and the company is measured according to its growth and profitability. Corporate CEOs are evaluated (and evaluate themselves) according to the growth and profits of the corporation they lead. Countries are evaluated according to their economic growth. Individuals are measured and evaluated (and measure and evaluate themselves) according to the money they make and possessions they accumulate.

Yet another important instrument of evaluation is position and power, or influence, as we often prefer to call it. One of the more tragi-comical elements in human interaction is the dance of people who just meet as they try to place one another on the scale of social position and influence through subtle questions and answers about such things as professions, schools attended and places of residence.

Power Rests on Fear

Yes, power ranks high on the evaluation scale. The old thought is permeated with thoughts of power. Power and our need for power is a reflection of fear that is born and nourished within the old thought. In the beginning, we are afraid of not "succeed-ing," not placing high enough on the evaluation scale. Having suc-ceeded to some degree, we are then afraid of losing what we have achieved and acquired, because our sense of security is based on our possessions and our position.

Those in power know the most about fear. They understand that fear is the greatest asset to maintaining power. That is why fear is such an important and widely used tool in corporations. (I have seen this from both sides. To my shame, I have used oth-ers' fear, and I have really felt fear myself.) Even our election campaigns are based on fear: "Vote for us, or you are risking your security."

Because fear causes suspicion and lack of trust (of ourselves and others), we build hierarchical systems for protection. The main function of hierarchies, as is explained in detail in Chapter 6, "About Hierarchies," is to ensure control, and the most important function of control is to prevent any threatening changes from taking place. In fact, each change we, ourselves, do not initiate is perceived as a threat.

Short-Term Thinking

The old thought is shortsighted. One of the more flagrant exam-ples is the way in which we—in the interest of the economy, in the interest of "growth"—treat nature. How often do we give pri-ority to the creation or preservation of job opportunities with no consideration of the resultant long-term and often irreparable damage to our surroundings and ultimately to ourselves?

Indeed, this perspective is not long term. Financial efforts are to a strikingly high degree more concerned with speculation than with investments in the usual sense, in order to build lasting substance. How often are corporate decisions made to meet financiers' demands of prompt return on investments rather than to meet the long-term needs of the corporations? How often do public corporations give priority to the performance of the shares on the stock exchange instead of to the needs of the corporations themselves? How often does the system (common everywhere in the industrialized world except, maybe, in Japan) of tying the salaries of CEOs and other chief executives to the profits of one year direct those executives to maximize the short-range profits at the cost of the long-term needs of the company? To satisfy the information needs of public shareholders we have introduced a system of quarterly reports, thereby enhancing the short-term focus even more; for many corporations the next quarterly report— and the stock exchange's reactions to that report—is more important than the appearance of the corporation two to three years ahead. Quarterly dividends in the U.S. (I have not seen it anywhere else) is the ultimate step in this direction.

Greed

The old thought is downright greedy. It is so greedy that often when the industrially developed nations of the world offer some of their abundance to help the Third World, the aid is given in a conditional form. ("We give this amount of money to you, but you must use it to buy goods and services from us.") This "aid" is used to buy markets. Yes, the old thought is so greedy that it allows banks and other financial institutions to lend money to Third World countries and then quietly watch how the borrowers, in order to pay only the interest on these loans, are forced to ruthlessly exploit their human and natural resources instead of building their societies.

Distance

The old thought creates distance. We have distanced ourselves from nature to the extent that we have completely lost our perspective. We consider ourselves to be the masters of nature and are exposing nature to reckless exploitation. By distancing ourselves from nature, we have created distances from and have lost contact with ourselves. The consequence is an everincreasing distance between humans: distance between parent and child, distance between citizen and government, distance between union member and union management, distance between employee and workplace.

In sum, the old thought is mechanical, emotionless and—as I think will become evident later in this book—hostile to life.

CHAPTER *4*

The New Thought

*T*he new thought is not a revolt against the old thought; its source is in the old way of thinking. We have outgrown the old thought. It is only now, having seen the old thought fully realized, that we can clearly understand that it will never lead to harmony, satisfaction or happiness, not even for those at the top.

I think the development of modern Sweden illustrates this.

At the turn of the century, conditions in Sweden were miserable and poverty prevailed. Only a small portion of the population (possibly five percent) enjoyed a standard of living that could be said to be decent. Class stratification and inequality were greater than what we now can imagine. Oppression was widespread. The right to vote was strongly limited. Few had access to a satisfactory education. Adequate health care was available only to a narrow circle. Social security did not exist. Children were auctioned by families who could not afford them. People who could not make a living because of illness or age had to suffer the shame of being put into the poorhouse. It was an unequal society, and the inequality had its base in material conditions.

I don't think it is difficult to picture the rage and the pain this situation must have caused. That rage and that pain gave birth to a vision of a new society and, considering the circumstances, it was only natural that this vision was primarily concerned with material well-being.

Carried by this vision, a number of people with a burning spirit accomplished in a remarkably short time an almost total transformation of Swedish society. Poverty was abolished. Democracy, once only a dream, was introduced. All people were given access to the education they wanted. Health care was made available. Security reforms (social welfare, health insurance, old age pension schemes, and so on) were implemented. By a consistent policy of income distribution, the country achieved almost total equalization of wealth and one of the highest standards of living in the world.

By and large, this change was accomplished by the middle of the 1960s. The vision of a new and "fair" society was fulfilled. Since then, the system has continued more or less automatically, with no clear vision to guide it. Instead of a vision, the system is perpetuated by a not-very-absorbing political power game. Now, the uphill road Sweden traveled until the middle of the 1960s has turned into an increasingly steep, downhill slide, resulting in the most materialistic country in the world (actually even more materialistic than the U.S.). Instead of creating a new vision and building a base for meaning, the present goal seems to be an expansion of the earlier goal: two cars instead of one, two houses instead of one (one in the city and one in the country), bigger boats and more possessions of all sorts. I do not think it an overstatement to say that Sweden today largely comprises dissatisfied, ever-complaining people, devoting much of their time trying to get as much as possible out of the government-provided welfare and security systems.

The Lost Perspective

As stated earlier, the means of attaining this vision were material. The vision was of economic-material opportunities, economic-material standards of living, economic-material security and conomic-material equalization. We Swedes were proud and happy to see our vision bearing fruit. We actually changed society; we actually saw improvements. But, as our thinking became so focused on the material aspects of our lives, we became obsessed with registering economical-material improvements at the expense of all else. We lost the human perspective, and our world view was severely limited.

We did not see that the vision was fulfilled. We did not see that continuing in the old and once so successful track was now leading us straight downhill. We did not see that it was time to change tracks, that it was time for a new vision.

Well, here we are. Sweden has reached a higher (material) standard of living than the Swedes ever dreamed possible. Most of us have been able to get those things—boats, cars, houses, electronic gadgets—that constitute the signs of abundance. And, as said above, one car or one house is no longer enough. The social security system is more or less suffocating the country and its inhabitants. Economical equalization has gone so far that some of its manifestations are almost comical. Each day we can see signs that we have pursued and are pursuing such a reckless exploitation of nature that we have brought ourselves to the verge of catastrophe.

Even so, economic growth continues to be Sweden's goal. We do not confine ourselves to merely protecting and greedily guarding our abundance. On top of that, we shall have more growth.

But now the questions come: Why should we have more growth? What shall be its source? Has what we have already accomplished led anywhere? Are we happier, are our lives more harmonious now than when this development started? Hasn't that freedom for which we searched turned into another form of captivity as we became the slaves of the economy? Aren't we possessed by our possessions and by our progress?

Are we really feeling that well? Aren't the ever-increasing drug abuse, use of prescription tranquilizers, youth riots, graffiti and employee absenteeism signs that we are doing badly, yes, really badly? Why don't we do anything about it? Why do we only patch a little here and there? Why do we concentrate on the symptoms instead of on the cause? Why do we say that we have to give more space for the "quality of life" without meaning it?

With these questions, we start outgrowing the old thought; the soil for a new vision is being prepared.

Sweden Is Not Unique

Even though I think that the development of modern Sweden well illustrates that we are about to outgrow the old thought, Sweden is not unique. Wherever I go in the Western world I see the same symptoms of disharmony, dissatisfaction and alienation. I see it in the other Scandinavian countries, in England, in Germany, in the Netherlands, in Switzerland, and in New Zealand.

And I see it in the U.S., where I have lived half of each year since 1987. I see graffiti. I see drug abuse. I see violence. All are symptoms of despair and alienation. I hear, more and more often, the questions: What is all this about? Do we really need or want just more of the same? Has the American Dream really made us happy, harmonious, satisfied? Isn't there more to the American Dream than just growth, material growth?

I see a growing alienation to the workplace ("I don't go there by choice but out of need"). I see more and more individuals leaving well-paid positions with large corporations—selling their Porsches and BMWs, moving their children from private to public schools—to take jobs in smaller companies ("Where I at least feel part of something whole") or to start their own business.

I feel a growing longing, yearning, for something else that, in many cases, is not yet identified.

This is just the beginning. As we start seeing through the system, start seeing that the system doesn't work anymore, our beliefs in the old system are shaken and a new belief system, a new set of values, emerges. A new vision is being born, not as a result of any organized movement—political, religious or otherwise—but as a result of an ongoing change within our minds, a change in our way of thinking.

Thus, between the two countries I know the best—Sweden and the U.S.—I don't see any differences in this respect. The political-economic history may differ, but the underlying thought has been the same: material growth. And in both countries the doubts are there, doubts as to whether once strongly held beliefs are still worth holding onto, are still meaningful.

A Total Shift in Our World of Thinking

Many of us have begun searching, searching for meaning. We have begun to see through the hollowness of our economic system. We have begun to see that the human aspects of work, business and economy have been lost in the shadows of our growth syndrome. We have begun to see that our economy and material progress do not serve people. In fact, it is the other way around. We have become prisoners of the economy, and we are on our way to consuming ourselves.

A new rage and a new pain is growing within us, and rage and pain will again give birth to a vision. The dimensions of this new vision are far wider than the vision born of the conditions in the beginning of this century. This new vision embraces our entire planet and all the humans living on it. It is a vision of compassion and humanity in the deepest sense of these words. It requires a total shift in our ways of thinking and perceiving.

The raising and stretching of human consciousness give birth to a new human and open the gates to our heretofore unsuspected inner resources. To see the new thought as a revolt is to make a fatal mistake, all the more important to emphasize because most of us feel there are good reasons for a revolt. But if we view the course of events as a revolt, we will inevitably fall into a defensive position. We will become frightened, start trying to protect the old ways and become even more rigid in our way of looking at things. Then we will not see that the development is passing us by. We will not adjust in time. Many now-vital companies will have painful awakenings, facing the fact that they have few, if any, possibilities for survival. This is a pity because living companies will be needed.

The New Thought Is Wholeness and Compassion

Central to the new thought is the realization that everything is part of a whole, that everything is interconnected. The new thought does not separate humans from nature. It does not make differentiations among humans. Every human is unique—has his or her distinctive features—and is, at the same time, part of every other human. In the new thought there is no concept of "we" and "they," only "we." And "we" is not only human beings. "We" is all life, including that which we cannot perceive with our five senses or explain with our intellects.

The new thought does not value anyone above another. It does not judge. It is tolerant. It represents compassion and humanity. The new thought sees and recognizes the dualism in humans: the (male) logical, thinking aspect and the (female) emotional, feeling aspect. In the new thought there is balance between these aspects. The emotional aspect, so oppressed in the old way of thinking, is now given equal weight. Logic is no longer dominant; logic and emotion are in union.

In the new thought we not only compute and calculate, we trust what our feelings are telling us. We do not need any other basis than our intuition for our decisions—our immediate apprehension or understanding. We *know*, we feel within us what is right and what is wrong.

In the new thought we do not set goals. We do not plan. We take our steps without knowing exactly where they will lead us. We do have expectations, but not specific ones. Life is not a complicated matter with which we have to wrestle and struggle. Life is more than a struggle to survive; it is one big adventure. Yes, every minute is an adventure. We see that every event—small or big, positive or negative—leads us forward.

At the core of the new thought is the concept that life is given to each of us for the sake of our personal and human development. Everything else—meaning all outer results—is secondary to that process this development constitutes. It is the process of life, of being itself, that is important, that is the meaning. It is in the process, not in the results of the process, that we develop.

In the new thought we begin to realize that we are creators. We are not at the whim of outer forces, not disabled victims of circumstance. What we experience, be it positive or negative, is a creation of our own thoughts. There is no good luck or bad luck, no chance.

To put this into the context of working life, we cannot say, "Had I not happened to have that boss, then . . ."; "Had I not happened to land in that company, then . . ."; "Had I not taken that job, then . . ."; "Had I not ended up with that partner, then. . . ." What occurs in our lives is all our own doing.

In the new thought there are no "musts." We do not do something because it is expected of us. We do what we want to do, what gives us joy, stimulation and meaning. Because the foundation of our actions is within us, our true resources can emerge.

The new thought also recognizes that every human being has much larger capacities than what we heretofore were able to imagine, that within every human lies a creativity that—given the right milieu—has hardly any limitations. To set free these inner resources and to allow this creativity to blossom is now the great challenge. Here lies the true potential for growth, for in the new thought, growth is not tantamount to outer, material growth but to personal and human growth.

It is in the process—by meeting challenges, problems and failures—that we develop both collectively and individually. It is in the process, not in the results of the process, that we attain new experiences, new insights and, finally, wisdom. **It is only when we succeed in uniting wisdom with the immense knowledge we have accumulated that we can reach our full human potential.**

Our companies now face what may well be their greatest challenge ever: to serve as the instruments of this process. To carry out this assignment, however, the companies will have to face their own challenges and go through their own existential crises.

CHAPTER *5*

About the Existential Crisis of Business

*A*lthough there are a growing number of exceptions, the companies of today are a reflection of the old thought. They are products of a pronounced logical, mechanical and materialistic way of looking at things. For me, the most striking expression is the way in which companies and employees regard each other. Each sees the other as a tool, and the association between employee and employer is mechanical.

This relationship could be said to be harmonious (or, as I will come back to in a moment, to have been harmonious) insofar as there is (or has been) an underlying, mutually agreed upon purpose: making money. In the old way of thinking, the primary purpose of work is to make money, and of business to make a profit. (It has seldom been expressed so bluntly as in the often-quoted statement by a former chairman of General Motors, who declared that the main purpose of GM was not to make cars but "to make profit.")

With this as a foundation, it isn't particularly remarkable that the business world we have built is nothing but a series of machines producing money distributed according to an ever more

29

complex system of laws and collective agreements. As I see it, there is no real life in the companies of today. They are not living entities within a living system.

Let us use nature as our model for a living system. Nature generates its own energy, and this energy is circulated within the system in exactly the right way. But the meaning of nature is not to produce energy. It produces only the energy needed to sustain and support the life process. And it is that process that is the meaning of nature.

Let us now regard the human being. We could say that the human being is an entity composed of a mind and a physical body, with the physical body acting as a vehicle for the mind. The mind expresses itself through the physical body as the body performs thoughts generated in the mind. It is in the mind that we develop and grow. It is where we record experiences, receive new insights and increase our knowledge. But without the physical body, development would be impossible.

In order to live, the physical body needs energy; ultimately, this energy is distributed as blood by the circulatory system. But the meaning of the human body is not to produce blood, and it does not produce more blood than it needs.

The meaning of the human body is that it should live to serve the mind as its vehicle or instrument. It is in the dimension of the mind that we develop and grow, not by making our bodies bigger. We grow inwardly, not outwardly.

To apply this analogy to a company: A company has a physical body in the form of machines, buildings, capital and so on. A company also has a mind composed of the human beings who work within the company. For its development and for its survival, the company needs energy, that is, profits or at least a positive cash flow. But is the meaning of the company the production of profits, the production of money?

I do not see it that way. Certainly, a company is as much in development as everything else. But it is not by expanding the outer shell that the company develops. That the buildings expand, the number of machines increases, the revenues grow, the capital multiplies, the holdings in other companies enlarge, the number of employees increases and so on, does not necessarily bring anything new into the picture—any more than if the human body continued to grow and grow. It is by inner expansion, by the development of its mind through new experiences, new insights and the increased knowledge of its employees, that development takes place. Everything else—profits, outer growth and so on—is a by-product.

This leads me to believe that the primary purpose of a company—its meaning—is to serve as an arena or vehicle for the personal and human development of those who are working in the company.

Companies Begin to Recognize the Human Mind and Its Resources, but, Paradoxically, the Gap between the Humans and the Companies Continues to Increase

It is true that during recent years businesses have started focusing more and more on the human mind and its resources. There is a growing understanding that human capacity and human creativity are much greater than was previously imagined. (Today it is a common opinion that we use only a small portion—some say about 10 percent—of our mental capacity.) Here and there it has become fashionable to say that employees are the most important resource of a company.

Even as the awareness of this thought grows and our inner resources become more accessible because of the steady rise and stretch of our consciousnesses, these resources are becoming more and more locked in instead of being let loose and allowed to blossom. The reason for this phenomenon is very simple and has to do with meaning.

The human mind is progressing beyond the old perception of the meaning of business. The human mind is continually growing, stretching, raising human consciousness. So what is happening is that individuals are changing and business has not caught up. Individuals are already absorbing the new thought. They are not focused on surviving, but rather on living and, by continuous development, reaching their full potential.

We no longer seek work based on possible earnings (and we have reason to thank our societies that we have reached that point). We no longer demand arenas in which we can obtain position and power. We demand arenas in which there are opportunities to develop our inner resources. Until we have such arenas, we unconsciously close the gates around our inner resources—we lock them in—because we feel they are not being used for something meaningful. Now we do not regard the production of money and subsequent over-consumption as meaningful but as meaningless.

As long as there is a gap between what people perceive as meaningful work and what companies perceive as meaningful business, it is of no help to say that employees are the most important resource of a company or to claim that human resources are far greater than we have heretofore perceived. It is of no help to make the workplace more physically comfortable or to design jobs to be more humane and attractive. And that gap not only exists, but it is widening and will continue to widen as people's search for meaning expands human consciousness. With this gap comes the alienation that most working people have begun to feel, perhaps without being able to pinpoint it. How often do we ask ourselves, "What am I actually doing?" For human creativity, and for the companies, there is hardly anything more devastating than this growing alienation. It leads to suffocation.

The big challenge for companies now is to become aware of the alienation and change the ground rules of business so they will correspond to the new thought, the new human. The purpose and meaning of companies must be redefined and brought into harmony with the thinking of human beings.

This is not an easy thing to do. We have to give up the old thought that is ingrained within us and is the very foundation on which we have based our existence. On top of that, we have to take on a new thought that is a glaring contrast to the old one.

Companies Must Transform Their Thinking

As hard as it may be to give up an old, ingrained thought, it is a vital prerequisite for the survival of companies that they change their thinking about their purpose to the following:

> The primary purpose of a company is
> no longer to make profit.
> Instead, the primary purpose of a company
> is to serve as an arena or platform
> for the personal and human development
> of those working in the company.

I hope it is clear from what I said previously that this does not imply that a company should not be profitable. Of course, companies of the future must generate the energy (profits) needed for survival. However, the main emphasis, the focus, is shifted from profitability to development: human development. Companies must become process oriented instead of results oriented.

By reaching that harmony between humans and companies, which can be achieved with the change to new thought, human resources are given a chance to emerge in full blossom. In this harmony, our extraordinary creativity can finally come through and do itself justice. In this harmony, the companies can become living entities.

With this transformation of thought—which implies that human concerns in all respects are placed above all else—changes follow in practically all aspects of business: the selection and design of products, the relationship with customers and clients, the relationship with competitors, the purpose and use of the profits generated by companies.

This turn of thought will also result in changes in the way companies are organized. The organizational forms of traditional companies have served as successful and constructive tools for implementing the purpose of the old thought. Now, in the new thought, these organizational forms become destructive obstacles to progress. I will come back to these matters.

CHAPTER 6

About Hierarchies

*I*n this chapter I argue that the prevalent hierarchical systems must be erased. It is my hope that after reading this chapter, you will clearly understand my reasons for this seemingly radical view.

First, I feel an urge to tell you about an experience that kicked me to deeply question our hierarchical systems and led me to this view, which is not that radical or revolutionary at all.

During the almost-ten years in top management of The Dagens Nyheter Group (now the Marieberg Group), Scandinavia's largest newspaper company, it took me almost all that time to fulfill one of my main assignments: to completely change the technology within the company. When I joined the company, practically every part of newspaper production (from the editorial rooms and advertising departments via the composing rooms to plate making, printing and distribution) was more or less what we today would call manual. The only area with some new technology was the accounting offices. When I left, the company was totally computerized.

It was a hell of a job and a fantastic challenge. It took all that time. Why? Because there was firmly rooted resistance to change.

Let me give you some details about the company: As a newspaper company it was large, with some 4,500 employees. It publishes two newspapers, which are totally separate editorially:

a daily morning paper with (at the time) a circulation of some 450,000 copies and a daily evening paper with a circulation of 600,000—650,000 copies. With the exception of a small amount of the evening paper, the two papers were entirely produced in the same building in Stockholm.

In that building there was more hierarchy, more defined territories, and more walls between people than I have experienced anywhere else. The production workers (called graphical workers) were divided into eight categories, each with its territory. And there was a ranking among these categories: the highest were the lithographers, the linotypers and the composers; the lowest, the mailroom workers. Over the workers presided a row of managers: supervisors and foremen, department managers, the production manager, the technical director and so on, all with their areas of command. On the editorial side was another long line of hierarchy. The journalists were divided into two groups, one for each newspaper. There were editorial supervisors and department managers up to the chief editors. Then there was the "business" side of each newspaper with its hierarchy: office workers and department managers up to the presidents. In fact, there was an invisible—but ever-present—wall between the newspapers themselves, competing for the facilities and other resources of the company. Finally, on top was the management of the entire concern trying to keep it all together.

When I first gave the signal of the necessity and our intention of introducing and implementing the new technology, I had not expected to be met with total excitement. But I had expected at least some genuine interest for the new, as a curiosity, if nothing else. Instead, literally every individual withdrew, wondering the same thing: "What does this mean for me?" The outcome of this process was total resistance, to some degree a blunt and outspoken resistance, but mainly a tacit resistance (with, indeed, very subtle ways of exercising it).

It did not take much to find out what had happened: the house was filled with fear. Wherever I went in the building I could sense—yes, almost see—this compact fear. It was not fear of losing jobs (early on we had made a commitment not to fire anybody as a result of the new technology). It was fear of losing achieved and established territories, group territories as well as individual territories. And the easiest way to prevent that from happening was to try to prevent any change.

I was not that concerned with the resistance. I knew we could find ways around it. But I was shaken by that immense fear. "Change," I said to myself, "is inevitable in every company, but must it necessarily be accompanied by fear? If that is the case, there must be something profoundly wrong with the human relations in our companies. And isn't it our hierarchical thinking that forms the very basis for how we relate, the fact that we think in terms of territories, positions and chains of command?"

I believe that anyone having experienced tangible fear as closely as I did would have reached the same conclusion I did: the hierarchical system, with all its implications, is devastating to the human being and to human progress. And here is my reasoning.

The hierarchical system provides the structure for our business organizations, and all activity within these organizations conforms to this superimposed pattern. This system encourages distances between coworkers, leads to inertia and inflexibility, and is devastating to creativity.

A Power Structure

The hierarchical system is a power structure in which certain individuals in an organization do not have any power, others have some power, and some have a great deal of power. Organizational charts carefully state who has power over whom, or—as it usually is expressed—who reports to whom. And in most companies, these charts of the power structure do not end with top management. Beyond these managers are the boards of directors and finally the shareholders. These individuals execute their power at shareholders' meetings. Majority shareholders, however, generally exercise their power in informal ways. It is common knowledge that many crucial business decisions are made without any close physical connection to the company in question—at a dinner table, in a meeting room at a bank office, at a board meeting of another company that owns a part of the company concerned. In a company fully or partly owned by the government, major decisions could be made at a government luncheon or at some informal meeting between a couple of cabinet members and their undersecretaries. Regardless, it is not uncommon that vital decisions concerning those companies are made by people who have never even seen the company.

There are also power holders who are not usually noted in organizational charts. They are nonetheless part of the hierarchy. I refer to collectives (labor unions) comprising individuals who have little power by themselves. These collectives, in turn, have their own hierarchy of power and exercise that power over their members. Some collectives (national unions) have power over other collectives (local unions), and so on.

These hierarchical systems are not the inventions of an elite sector of our societies. They are a characteristic of our culture—indeed, of every culture—and are in no way unique to the world of business. The institutions of our culture—our public bureaucracies, our churches, our armies—are hierarchically organized. Throughout recorded history, power has been accepted as a natural element of all parts of our societies.

What is being called into question is not power, as such, but the distribution of that power. Even in the most progressive society, power has always been supported by rationales such as "Those who have the responsibility also need the power to be able to execute that responsibility" or "In the common interest of us all, someone must have power."

By not questioning power itself but only the distribution of power, we accept, de facto, the hierarchical system. (Every redistribution of power surely leads to new hierarchies. We only have to look at the history of revolutions to see that.) Regardless of where we may be on the hierarchical scale, we all are responsible for the existence of our hierarchical systems. We legitimize them with our ways of thinking.

Our Need for Power

It is easy to understand how we support these hierarchical systems with our thinking if we look at what is behind our need for power. We have already touched on that subject in Chapter 3, "The Old Thought." I would like to expand this topic by pointing to some concurrent—and not detachable—elements of our way of thinking that constitute the foundation of hierarchical systems.

Characteristic of our old, logical way of thought is the compulsion to categorize, evaluate and measure human beings in material terms. We place human beings in boxes and identify people, ourselves included, not according to who they are, but according to what they do for work and their social and material accomplishments. In all this, there is an inherent need to climb upward on the scale. For each little step we take, we gain something to protect and secure. While jealously guarding what we have obtained we strive to secure a platform to advance and climb further.

There is also an inherent fear, a fear of losing what we have obtained and of not being able to climb further. We therefore seek power to secure the best possible control over situations that may expose us to any risk of being stopped, or of losing what we have obtained. The more we have obtained, the more we have to lose; the more we have to lose, the greater our fear; the greater our fear, the greater our need for power. It is not only our livelihoods or our positions at stake; it is our very identities.

Power is the other face of fear. The hierarchical system is a power structure built upon fear and, by extension, upon suspicion and mistrust.

This entire construct emanates from our way of thinking, from our categorizing, evaluating and measuring. Ultimately, its origin can be found in the distances we have created among individuals. These distances are not only manifested in the hierarchical systems, but they are reinforced by them.

In the new thought—which tells us that every human being is not only unique, but also is a part of every other human being—no such distances exist. There is no competition among human beings. There is no fear of not being successful, no fear of losing. In the new thought, there is no need for power and no room for hierarchical systems. The new thought and hierarchical systems are simply not compatible.

Now, let us shift our focus from the causes of the hierarchical system to its effects.

The Hierarchical System is an Impediment to Development and Leads to a Waste of Energy

I don't think it is particularly difficult to see that the hierarchical system is an impediment to development and a waste of energy. I have to admit, though, it is much easier for me to see this from my present perspective than it was during the period when I was an active participant in the hierarchical power-position game. The hierarchical system, by necessity, encourages individuals to devote much of their time and energy to protecting and improving their positions. This guarding of territory within all levels of hierarchies wastes more power and energy than we generally imagine.

Whether consciously or unconsciously, explicitly or implicitly, people in hierarchical systems act in ways that best serve their own interests; hierarchies create competition for positions of power. And, the higher in the hierarchy we look, the more evident the competition, because there are fewer positions for which to compete.

The energy wasted by competition and by guarding of positions is not necessarily the result of direct, overt actions. Most often the waste is the product of small, hardly noticeable deviations from the course. And these deviations are there. They cannot be avoided.

Picture a big ship on its course from the harbor to the open sea. The ship is surrounded by small, fiery tugboats, each with its tow line to the ship. Think of the energy and force that would be generated if all the tugboats were pulling in the same direction! Consider the situation if the tugs refrain from towing and just stay beside the ship, protecting their individual positions while the ship attempts to make its way under its own power. Then picture the tugs pulling in different directions. Much power is generated and deployed by all the tugs, but the forces cancel each other out. All the collective power leads nowhere and the energy is wasted.

Hierarchy Means Inertia

Inertia is inherent in a hierarchy. A system based on fear, suspicion and lack of trust naturally resists change; every change is perceived as a threat. When faced with a possible change, anyone within a hierarchy will first ask "What does this mean for me?" rather than "What does this mean for the company?"

How much time and how much energy is wasted trying to answer this question? When answered, how much time and how much energy is then used to resist the change or to modify it to suit one's own interests and to strengthen one's own position?

Hierarchy Is Devastating to Creativity

Let us now consider an area in which the hierarchical model has truly devastating effects: human creativity.

Before addressing this issue, I would like to quote Tom Melohn, former president and CEO (or Head Sweeper, as he preferred to call himself) of North American Tool and Die, a metal stamping company in the San Francisco Bay Area. Melohn took over the company in the late 1970s and, in 1990, sold it to his employees. During his tenure as president, sales grew twenty-eight percent compounded annually. Pretax earnings increased 2,400 percent, and productivity, 480 percent. Absenteeism decreased to less than one percent and turnover to less than four percent. All this, Melohn explained (*The New Partnership*, Managing for Excellence with Tom Melohn, A Video Case Study Enterprise Media 1990), was the result of uncompromised adherence to five basic principles: honesty, trust, mutual respect, openness and creativity.

Tom Melohn has this to say about creativity:

> You generally think about artists and writers. But I think creativity can be anything. Our toolmakers take a great big piece of steel and make it into an absolute jewel, with tolerances of one thousand to an inch. That's creativity. Our engineers take a dumb blueprint and read it and design a die that will make

a part that has a tolerance of less than one-fourth the thickness of a human hair. That's creativity.

Yes indeed, creativity can be anything. Creativity can and should be part of every aspect of our lives. Creativity can and should be part of our work, regardless of whether that work is labeled as blue collar or white collar.

Company managers are beginning to see the importance of creativity in the workplace. They sense that only a small portion of available human resources is being used and demand creativity from workers. Those responsible for the operation of companies hope to use the largest possible portion of our untapped mental capacities, and they look for ways to stimulate creativity.

Often, however, they begin by mistakenly thinking that increased creativity means increased profitability or outer growth. They overlook the fact that the individuals whose unused creativity they wish to exploit are no longer motivated by profitability. We are seeing a growing gap between the focus of companies on profits and the focus of employees on personal development.

The focus on outer growth inevitably leads to the invention of economic incentives (rewards) for employees to use their hidden inner resources. Companies have also began investing in what could be called "creative milieus": hanging paintings on the walls and designing buildings and work areas to be stimulating to creative thinking. Unfortunately, these efforts are usually concentrated in the office areas where, for some reason, it is believed there is more creativity to be used or expressed than in the workshop areas. And though these efforts are laudable, they miss the point. As long as we cling to the hierarchical model and thereby maintain an efficient barrier to the development of creativity, such efforts are essentially wasted.

What Is Creativity?

Let us examine the nature of creativity. The subject is now attracting much attention and more and more definitions of the word are coming forward. One is this: "Creativity is the solving of a problem without having the means of the solution at hand."

A perhaps more comprehensive definition is this: "Creativity means to meet challenges, solve problems and accept failures, thereby obtaining new knowledge and new insights."

The definition, however, that best agrees with my understanding is this: "Creativity is that process through which we, by meeting challenges and solving problems, reach the insight that our capacity is larger than what we believe it to be."

There is gold to be found in facing challenges and problems, regardless of success or failure. With these thoughts in mind, it is easy to see that creativity and hierarchy are not compatible.

The development of our creativity presupposes that we test our capacity. Not only must we be given the opportunities to test ourselves, but also we must accept those opportunities given us. How could we obtain insights about our capacities without testing? A hierarchical system built upon fear, suspicion and lack of trust offers little incentive for such testing.

Challenges

Usually, there is little inclination to offer real challenges to employees in the lower levels of business hierarchies. It would require some freedom to meet those challenges, and someone higher up would have to relinquish some control. Control is the tool with which position is guarded and maintained. To offer a challenge, the person in charge would have to ask, "Do I have enough faith in myself to let go of some of my fortifications? Can I trust the recipient not to make use of this opportunity to improve his or her position? And what will happen if he or she fails? Ultimately, I will have to bear the responsibility. Isn't it better that I do it myself? In any case, I cannot give away the control." This line of thought probably ends with, "And if I delegate this assignment, I will set up a framework to keep my control."

The one who receives such an assignment is also in a difficult position. On the one hand, to pass up the opportunity would have negative consequences for future advancement. On the other hand, failure would also have a negative effect on future opportunities in the organization. In addition to the fear of failure, the person is well aware of the lack of freedom within the situation and feels that "they don't really trust me up there."

This is certainly not a creative milieu. It is highly unlikely that, under such circumstances, people could acquire the balance, harmony and faith in self necessary to reveal the hidden resources that would allow them to achieve the "impossible."

Problems

Let us look at how problems are dealt with in hierarchies. Problems are a type of challenge, but they have a somewhat different life than the challenges we've been discussing.

Problems arise; they arise regardless of where we happen to be within the hierarchy. The interesting thing is how we deal with them, because we would rather not have them at all. We are afraid of them. We are not sure if we can solve them, at least not to the satisfaction of our superiors. We cannot be absolutely sure of what our superiors really think. Because there *is* a risk of failure, we do what we can to avoid taking any action.

Problems, unlike challenges, are fairly easy to avoid. We can hide them, let them stay with us, put them in the pile of papers on our desks and hope that they will solve themselves. We can make some change to make the problem less evident, thus sparing ourselves from having to address it "right now." If we cannot hide the problem, we can always push it away from us, upward in the organization. "Those up there have the final decision, anyway. The best thing to do is to let them take care of it." So we push the problem a step or two up in the hierarchy.

At the higher level, other attempts are made to hide the problem or to just sit on it. Finally, something must be done and the problem is again pushed upward until it finally comes to "those up there." They don't want it either, but now it can't be pushed up further. They may try to sweep it under the carpet, but one day a solution will be required. Then begins the process of pushing the problem downward within the hierarchy. Finally, it gets back to where it started, and a new round begins.

During my time with the Dagens Nyheter Group, I experienced this phenomenon in very direct ways. The building that houses the company's operations was constructed in the 1950s and has a hierarchical structure. Its form is a tower, a rather narrow and rather high tower, that rests upon a boxlike "industrial" building where the technical production of the newspapers takes place. This building has three floors above and three floors below the ground. The tower has twenty-five floors with the top two floors housing service equipment. The twenty-third floor is the so-called executive-entertainment floor, and top management is located on the twenty-second floor.

I was responsible for departments located from the third floor underground up to the twenty-first floor in the tower. A problem would arise in the pressroom (third floor underground) and would first be pushed up to the pressroom management on floor one. From there it moved to the production management on floor three and then to the technical management on floor sixteen. From there, the problem would be pushed to personnel management on floor fifteen. From floor fifteen the problem would then come to me on floor twenty-two.

I did not want it. If I was unsuccessful in my attempts to push it a last step upward, I would begin to push it downward. Eventually, and sometimes sooner than later, the problem would come back to me accompanied by strong union demands for a solution. It would continue wandering up and down for some time until a solution could no longer be avoided.

The solution, however, rarely came from where the problem first arose and, as a result, nothing was learned. The "gold" that originally existed within the problem was mostly lost.

I often wished that those problems could have taken the forms of bright lights, so that if we had stood on the street in front of the building, we could have visually followed them on their journeys up and down the hierarchy.

Problems can indeed have an exciting and varied life within a hierarchical system. More time is used to shove a problem back and forth, up and down, than is actually used to solve it. When a solution finally comes forth, it is often a forced, emergency solution, not one resulting from a process of balance, harmony and true creativity.

Problems Are a Gift

In a hierarchical system, problems are not taken care of in a proper way. They are not seen as gifts given to the one who is first presented with the problem and who is closest to the solution. A problem arising on the third floor underground is best solved there and not on the twenty-second floor above ground. (When the implementation of a solution calls for a decision to be made "higher up," such as resource allocation, the issue is a different one. In that case, the solution, not the problem, is pushed up in the organization.)

Problems constitute a gift. When I address a problem—on my own or in cooperation with others—I actually become the solution. I see that I am more, and I grow. Furthermore, I don't do someone a favor by solving his or her problem. To solve another's problem is, in fact, one of the greatest disservices we can possibly render.

In Conclusion

The hierarchical system is a power structure. It is built upon fear, suspicion and lack of trust. It reinforces the distance among individuals and thoroughly prohibits creative cooperation by creating a climate of competition. It is an impediment to development and leads to wasted energy. It builds inertia and inflexibility into our organizations and is devastating to our creativity.

We will never realize our full potential as human beings unless hierarchies are abandoned.

CHAPTER 7

More about Hierarchies

We all know that energy is being wasted in our organizations, that hierarchical systems create inertia and resistance to change, that these systems discourage us from giving and accepting challenges while they encourage us to avoid facing problems. Nevertheless, we do not take corrective steps to erase the hierarchies from our organizations. True, we have begun to question the system and have started talking about flattening out our organizations, that is, decreasing the number of levels. In practice, this essentially means that we cut down on middle management levels and retain the basic structure. But does that lead anywhere?

By decreasing the number of middle levels, we might temporarily blow some new life into an organization, but in the long run we rarely accomplish anything except, perhaps, lowering wage costs. It is not the number of levels within an organization that causes the damage, but our hierarchical way of thinking. We don't remove fear, suspicion and lack of trust by decreasing the number of levels if we still think in terms of a power structure. We still evaluate ourselves and others according to position.

What we are doing in these attempts is seizing a new, valuable thought and incorporating it into the old way of thinking. We still cling to the hierarchical system and do not dare to let it go completely. This reluctance is easy to justify as long as we seek our identity outside ourselves, as long as we see ourselves as "someone" by virtue of our position and possessions. For those who have obtained something, abolishing the hierarchy would put their identity at risk. For those who have not yet started their climb, abolishing would remove the entire arena of possible achievement.

It is our world of perception that we have to change. If we stop evaluating each other in material terms, if we see that everyone has inherent value, if we make no distinctions among people, and if we see that our identity and security lie within us, then abolishing the hierarchy does not mean that we will be forced from our positions or, if we have not yet started our climb, that we will be excluded and left with no motivation. Abolishing the hierarchy would be a move toward new opportunities of personal development for all. We have nothing real to lose, but much to gain.

All of us at times have understood this idea and have touched upon these lines of thought. Yet, most of us have blocked them and have not let them take hold because they frighten us. It is frightening to leave the familiar, even though we feel it is wrong, for something unknown.

Nonetheless, this change is unavoidable. Either we voluntarily make the change ourselves or it will be made for us. Abolishing hierarchies is unavoidable, because it is happening as the result of a change in thought already taking place. This change is not something we can neglect or treat as a revolt and try to crush. This new thought is a natural phase of human development that is growing by its own force. It is a development that may be slowed a little, but not stopped. An indication of this change of thought is the growing number of employees who break away from "old" companies to establish new ones based on the new way of thinking and organized without hierarchies.

Although we are all close to the new way of thinking, those high up in hierarchies who feel they have much to lose will be inclined to cling to the old thought and resist change. The higher the position, the greater the resistance. Ultimately, those attempting to preserve the hierarchical model will be the subjects of change that comes from below. They will watch the old way of thinking—and the hierarchical system with it—literally being pushed out from the bottom. Moreover, they will experience greater and greater difficulties recruiting labor as more and more people choose not to give time and energy to companies controlled by the old thought. This will force companies to choose between perishing or implementing change.

When I discuss with friends and colleagues abolishing the hierarchical system, the main objection can be paraphrased as follows: "What you are saying sounds fine. But is it possible in practical life, in practical business life? Yes, true, we can see the negative affect of hierarchies, but even if we fully adopt the new way of thinking, is it really possible to run a company with no hierarchy? Someone has to have final say; someone has to take responsibility. Can one have responsibility without power?"

I believe it is possible to run a company without hierarchies. Why shouldn't it be possible to have companies in which everyone is responsible, and equally so? Why should such companies be beyond our conceptual capacities?

Of course the absence of a hierarchy does not eliminate the need for leaders or managers of specific tasks, of the overall operations of the company or the departments within it. The leaders in new companies, however, are different from traditional leaders in that they are not appointed on the basis of power. The characteristics of this new leadership are discussed in the following chapter.

CHAPTER 8

About Leaders
and Coordinators

*I*n the new company, everyone as I stated earlier, is responsible, and equally so. No hierarchy exists; there is only one level. Nevertheless, there are leaders.

Leadership within the new companies differs markedly from what we have traditionally meant by leadership or management. The decisive difference lies in the way leaders are appointed. Leaders in traditional companies are appointed from power to power.

In the traditional company, the leader is appointed to power by those in power. The power emanates from the ownership and the owner(s) appoint the ultimate management: the board of directors. In so doing they see to it that the composition of the board best reflects the interests of the owner(s). This loyalty is almost more important than how competent board members are.

The directors represent the interest of the owner or a certain owner. Thus, for instance, someone who purchases a considerable amount of stock in a company will expect to be represented on the board of directors.

In the case of a subsidiary company, the board will often consist of top executives from the parent company; the owners delegate power to the board of the parent company and no further. It is the board of the parent company that makes the decisions crucial to the life of the subsidiary company, not the subsidiary company's board.

The board of directors elects the company's executive management. These appointments are also based on the specific interests the directors represent. For instance, in joint ventures or other arrangements with more than one owner group, agreements are often made in which one owner group appoints the chairman of the board while another owner group appoints the president and CEO. On the basis of the interests they are expected to protect, these executive managers then appoint the managers on the next level beneath them. These managers then appoint their closest collaborators, and so on to the bottom of the organizational hierarchy. Thus, a thread of owner interests runs down through the entire organization. This is a natural consequence of the hierarchical power structure.

In certain countries it is now a common custom (in Sweden and Germany it is a law) that the appointment of managers be preceded by consultations with those who are to work under those managers. The appointment itself, however, and for that matter any dismissal, is accomplished in conformity with the hierarchical order on the basis of power.

In the New Company Leaders Are Not Appointed

In the new company, leaders are not appointed, nor are they chosen. Are they then elected by their coworkers? No, I don't think so. An election procedure presupposes that someone presents himself or herself as a candidate to the post in question and then conducts some sort of "election campaign." Moreover, this presupposes that there are positions in the company considered to be more important or attractive than others. Not in the new company—all work assignments are equally important.

Leadership in the new company is formed by mutual consent. Individuals are called upon by colleagues to serve them as leaders of their operations or assignments, and they accept or reject those responsibilities.

What Does Leadership in the New Company Imply?

What does it mean to be a leader in the new company? To begin with, a leader has no external power and is not at the top of the organization. He or she is in its midst. A leader does not decide issues except when explicitly asked. A leader does not give orders and does not even lead. A leader coordinates the overall operation, or parts thereof.

In the new company there are no "bosses," nor are there any leaders in the traditional sense. These functions are replaced by coordinators.

The responsibilities of coordinators are broader than those of traditional leaders, because basic to the new company is the fact that employees are not there to serve the company. On the contrary, the company is there to serve the employees as a platform for their personal development. Therefore, the tasks of the coordinator are not limited to making sure the activities he or she coordinates are running smoothly. A substantial part of the assignment is to ensure that the activities being coordinated are serving those who are performing the activities. That is, the organization and its activities furnish, to as large an extent as possible, the best opportunities for personal development to all employees.

Finally, the coordinator disperses information. A coordinator sees to it that all employees whose activities are being coordinated are kept informed and that information about the activities for which an employee is responsible are known in other parts of the company. As discussed in the following chapter, total openness is one of the cornerstones of the new company; everyone in the company has access to all information.

Who Becomes a Coordinator?

Who then, is asked to be a coordinator? It would be natural to turn to someone with the most experience—not the least of which would be life experience—and who is a good judge of human nature. By using these criteria, however, there is a danger of developing a pattern of seeking the one considered to have the best qualifications for the task. In so doing we again run the risk of encouraging a kind of elite corps ("professional coordinators") to emerge. Then we will not only soon find ourselves back in a hierarchical system, but also we will do ourselves a disservice. Why? Because, if those who are good coordinators spend the main part of their lives performing this function, they will miss the challenges and growth supplied by the very assignments for which they believe themselves to be less qualified. In addition, if "coordinatorship" is reserved for a small circle, then the great majority would be excluded from that opportunity for personal development.

This applies to all assignments in an organization. Because the function of the workplace is to serve as a platform for personal development, one could say—somewhat incisively—that the interests of a company are best served if work assignments are given to those who believe themselves to be least suited for them. Those tasks contain the greatest challenges. Job rotation, therefore, will be an important and natural element in the new company. All work assignments are equally important, and one job is no more attractive than another. Jobs will be exchanged, and it will be the task of the coordinator to see that the coordinatorship rotates as well.

Good Leaders and Good Coordinators

In the old way of looking at business, much effort has been devoted describing the characteristics of a good manager or leader. That ideal has changed from time to time. During some periods, leaders were supposed to be technically minded, during other periods, more market oriented. Sometimes, leaders were expected to be some kind of superpeople who worked long days, had computers for brains, and were hard-nosed. During other periods, leaders were expected to be soft and easygoing. Sometimes, leaders have been general targets to shoot at and ridicule. At other times, they have been heroes.

It would be wrong, however, to define what characterizes a good coordinator in the new way of looking at business. One could possibly try to define a good coworker in a business organization, but that also feels wrong. Why? Because we are discussing human beings, not human beings in a certain situation. So, what we are really searching for is a definition of a good human being. From that I abstain. I will confine myself to establishing that the new human being listens, tries to understand fellow humans' situations, and looks for the good in everyone.

CHAPTER 9

About Organization

Much time and energy has been devoted to finding the perfect organization for the traditional company. The ideas about what such an organization should look like have changed from time to time, and distinct schools or models—line-staff, matrix, and so on—have emerged. They have not, however, been all that different from one another: they have all been based on the hierarchical model that minutely describes the chains of command and the power structure.

This fascination with models will not likely occur with the new companies because they will not have a set organizational form. The way businesses are organized will vary from company to company and will probably depend more on the type of people working there than on the type and scope of the activities performed. The structures of the new companies can change and evolve as needed, because the resistance to change found in hierarchical systems will be absent. In the new company, the organizational form will not be a state, but a process.

Even though there is no given or typical organizational form for the new company, I believe these forms will have some common traits, namely closeness, openness and flexibility.

Closeness

As discussed earlier, one of the cornerstones of the new way of thinking is the belief that everything is interconnected and constitutes a unity; there are no distances. This belief will be reflected in different ways by the organizational forms we choose. In those forms, we will eliminate distances and aim at closeness—closeness among humans in the organization, closeness between humans and their companies, closeness to work assignments, and closeness to external interested parties such as customers, suppliers and the community where the company is located.

A big step toward closeness has already been taken by abolishing the hierarchical system. Our drive for closeness will also be furthered by two things: making our organizations smaller and by reducing the number of middlemen.

It has been suggested that the development toward smaller organizations would necessarily mean that only what we call small businesses have a future. Even if it is there that we will see the first changes and will marvel at the vitality being developed, large corporations are not necessarily doomed to die. Closeness and togetherness could also be achieved in larger companies.

When it comes to huge corporations—the "dinosaurs," the difficulties in adjusting to the new era will be so great that I doubt they will survive. For these companies, I can see no other means of survival than the rapid breakdown into small, interdependent unities in which the real process of change and readjustment can take place.*

---

*There are numerous theories about the sudden extinction of dinosaurs some seventy million years ago. Common to all such theories is these giant creatures' lack of adaptation to rapid change. One interesting explanation for the lack of adaptability has a biological basis: The dinosaurs had been using so much power and energy

I do believe, however, that it is possible to achieve closeness in business units larger than what we call small businesses. Only experience can tell us where the upper limit may be. One way for businesses of greater size to achieve closeness is to become project oriented or network organizations.

In a network organization, the people working on each project form a network. These networks, when combined, form a larger network. The larger networks could then form a yet larger network, and so on. What keeps the organization together is not an all-powerful board or executive management team making all the decisions. What keeps it together is a commonly shared vision. The activities within and between the individual projects is monitored by coordinators. The need for closeness will in itself keep the number of persons within a project relatively low.

Some companies have already organized along these lines. The Swedish computer consulting company ENATOR is one example. This company, founded in 1977, is organized into several separate companies (projects, if you will) and has grown rapidly. When the operations in one company grow so that more than 50 persons are employed, a new company is created, because those working together in one company should be given a real chance to know each other more comprehensively than is normally the case. This has many benefits. For instance, when allocating different assignments, knowledge of the employees enables the project coordinator to take into account employees' technical competence as well as their character strengths and personal conditions.

---

building brain function capable of controlling the mass of muscles in their giant bodies that they neglected to develop their awareness. The degree of awareness—consciousness—had not reached a level capable of perceiving and adjusting to rapidly changing conditions.

The U.S. company W. L. Gore & Associates Inc. (Gore), the manufacturer of Gor-Tex, also saw early on the importance of closeness and of keeping the number of employees relatively low. As described further in Chapter 16, "On Our Way," Gore is focused on innovation. It practices a unique management system (the Lattice System) designed to encourage direct person-to-person contacts and transactions. Since its start in 1958, the company has had very rapid growth. Yet none of its plants (forty-six as of spring 1992) is allowed to exceed 150 to 200 workers. In Gore's experience, as soon as a plant grows to that size, the direct person-to-person system tends to break down. The company therefore assumes the extra expense of building another plant.

Another example of a company working to keep units relatively small is Semco S/A, Brazil's largest marine and food-processing machinery manufacturer. (For a more detailed description, see Chapter 16, "On Our Way.") In an article in the *Harvard Business Review* (September–October 1989), Semco's president, Ricardo Semler, offered these thoughts about the subject:

> For more than five million years, they [our ancestors] refined their ability to work in groups of no more than about a dozen people. Then along comes the industrial revolution, and suddenly workers are trying to function efficiently in factories that employ hundreds and even thousands. Organizing those hundreds into teams of about ten members each may help some, but there's still a limit to how many small teams can work well together.

Ricardo Semler's and Semco's conclusion is that the upper limit of an efficient production unit is about 150 people.

In the context of old business life, there is a great distance among people. One contributing factor is the system of so-called middlemen: persons or functions standing between functionaries, thereby blocking many of those direct contacts so important for personal development. Although this was not the original purpose of creating middlemen, this distance is the result of it. This hinders the development of contact among people; it hinders opportunities wherein creativity could blossom.

If we took the time to look closely, we could see a striking number of middlemen functions. First of all, we have middlemen standing in the way of direct contacts within companies. Each management level within a hierarchy functions as a middleman. Rules, both written and unwritten, determine how questions can be properly addressed upward (and, for that matter, downward) in organizations. Those in charge of the levels within the hierarchy will react strongly if passed over. The number of direct contacts between top management and the people on the floor are, for instance, very few. It is easy to imagine how good ideas are lost or changed as they pass through the middlemen before reaching their destinations.

Middlemen are also found in the so-called expert functions (staff functions) of a company. For instance, personnel matters are supposed to be referred to a special personnel functionary for disposition instead of being solved directly by those involved in the matter. Should that matter involve a union issue yet another middleman, the union, becomes involved.

Another example is the purchasing department. In companies with purchasing departments, people who need equipment must deal with two middlemen, their immediate supervisors and the purchasing department, who stand between them as buyers and suppliers of the goods in question.

The number of middlemen within companies will decrease (and may even vanish) with the abolishment of the hierarchical model. But we also have a great number of middlemen standing between companies and their external interested parties such as customers, suppliers and community members.

The greatest number of middleman functions are found in the areas of sales and marketing. It is normal for practically all companies of some size to have special sales and marketing departments. These departments function as the first link between the people manufacturing a product and the people buying and using it. More than likely other links are involved: local sales offices, general agents with subagents, and, finally, the retailers. Additionally, information about the product—and often the creation of the buyer's need for it—is handled by yet another middle-link: advertising agencies.

We will probably see a rapid and extensive decrease of these middlemen as well, not only for reasons of cost (in many cases these middlemen functions account for the largest price component), but also as a result of our seeking more direct contact, more closeness. As buyers, we want to be able to contact whoever manufactured the product directly. As manufacturers, we want direct contact with those buying and using our products.

Some car manufacturers, Volvo for instance, have begun to abandon assembly line production for teams that manufacture a car from beginning to end. I don't think it is totally impossible for a car buyer, before and during the course of manufacturing, to be in direct contact with those making his or her car. Such direct contact would probably encourage the creation of cars that are better than ever.

We have already started seeking forms of selling and buying without middlemen or with as few middlemen as possible. The rapid growth of small, local grocery markets—farmers' markets— where producers sell their products directly to consumers, is one example of this development. Other examples are small, often specialized, mail order companies and trade fairs of different kinds. I have discovered companies that have totally abolished their sales and marketing departments and are instead concentrating solely on trade fairs (Skaltek AB, described in Chapter 10, "About Goals, Plans and Visions," is one of them). They are not sending sales staffs to these fairs, but rather are sending those individuals directly responsible for the products: the designers, fabricators and assemblers.

Openness

A lasting impression from my time in the traditional business world is the cult of secrecy where information and activities had to remain hush-hush. We concealed information for reasons of competition. We concealed information for tactical reasons. We concealed information in order not to create suspicion or apprehension. We concealed information for stock exchange reasons and so forth.

Of course, there were (and are) situations in which the classified stamp is needed, but I felt it was becoming an almost automatic procedure, as when meetings were closed with words such as, "We should keep this to ourselves until further notice" or "This must not leak out." The classified stamp was used, often by me, without any deep reflection and for no substantial reason. I think the real motive for creating so much classified material was to bestow a feeling of exclusivity or specialness to the informed circle.

In the old company, there are rules about who has the right to give information or to comment about the company and its activities. Sometimes there are public relations departments and public relations officers (yet another middleman function) assigned to filter and direct information released to the outside.

The new company is an open company: there are no secrets. In a company where no distinctions are made among people, where everyone is equally responsible, every person has access to all information. Access to information is not formalized, but instead goes directly from the source to the one who asks for it. This allows people to be in direct contact with each other. Openness in the new company is encouraged not only in its internal workings but also in its relations with the surrounding world.

Some may object that total openness is unrealistic. After all, there must be some circumstances in which strong restrictions on information are necessary, such as those involving competitors or, in the case of public companies, complying with rules imposed by stock exchange ethics. Regarding competitors, I daresay that this need will disappear. In the world of the new thought, there will be a totally new way of looking at competition.

In the world of the new thought, everything begins with the human being. Every human being is considered unique and completes (not competes with) every other human being. Companies consist of human beings; these human beings *are* the companies. Consequently, every company is unique and completes, not competes with, other companies. This is true regardless of how similar the activities of companies may be. In the new thought, competition will not be sufficient reason to keep information secret.

An interview I heard on a radio news program in August 1989, provides a brutal example of where competitive thinking leads us. This story concerned the discovery by a laboratory jointly owned by Swedish paper mills of a production method that decreased energy consumption by fifty percent. The energy savings provided by this process would be of tremendous benefit to the paper mills, to the country as a whole and even to the entire planet, because one of the most energy-intensive industrial processes involves the production of one kind of paper pulp produced in many parts of the world.

Yet, the laboratory representative being interviewed was unwilling to describe the new method for fear of giving it to the pulp industries of other countries. The Swedish pulp industry did not want to share the discovery because it wanted to keep ahead of the competition. It was of no concern that the discovery would be of great benefit to the people of other countries whose energy sources were being drained by their pulp industries.

There are already today, in the U.S., in Sweden and probably in other parts of the world, companies practicing total openness toward customers as well as other companies involved in the same business. These companies practice the open book system. Anyone can study their accounts, their outgoing and incoming invoices, and get a clear picture not only of the net worth of the company but the profitability of certain products or services as well.

As for the secrecy imposed by the rules governing publicly owned companies, such rules have increased in number and scope to keep pace with the growing speculative elements in our economy. The need for these rules will remain as long as our present economic system and forms of company ownership remain unchanged. Considerable changes are inevitable in these areas, however, and I discuss them in Chapters 14 and 15, "About Ownership" and "About the World Economy."

Flexibility

The third common trait of organizational forms of our new companies is flexibility. The foundation for flexibility has been laid by abolishing the hierarchical system. As a result, there is no longer fear of or subsequent resistance to change. Now, the basic motivation is no longer that we should climb as far as possible and amass as much money as possible. Now, resistance to change has been replaced by its opposite. In our striving for personal development, we will demand changes as we seek new challenges and face new problems.

The organization of the new company is not a fixed state, but a process in which people and activities are consistently grouped and regrouped to provide the best possibilities for creative work. When routine creeps into work assignments, when we start feeling secure in our positions, when we no longer have that little anxiety about what we are supposed to do, then we will know it is time to change. And we will make those changes, within as well as among companies.

CHAPTER 10

About Goals, Plans and Visions

*I*n the old way of thinking there is a strong tendency to evaluate. To evaluate, criteria or yardsticks are needed. When a business is evaluated, the most commonly used yardsticks are profits, market shares and productivity. Because in the old, linear way of thinking bigger is better, growth is the all-important yardstick.

Those who lead companies are evaluated according to these same yardsticks. Most business managers want to be evaluated as highly as possible, so they naturally strive to achieve the best possible results for their companies. The driving force to achieve results is strong, indeed. The goals typically set for businesses are a consequence of these ambitions. These goals are called such names as marketing objectives and profit projections.

These goals are normally set once a year for a period of one year. Although it is becoming more common to plan for longer periods, goals beyond the next fiscal year are rare. Reaching the goals is considered good performance; not reaching them is regarded as failure. Surpassing the goals is counted as superior performance. Therefore, consciously and unconsciously, goals are set so that there is a good chance of reaching and, preferably, surpassing them.

I imagine that in most companies, the annual budget follows similar procedures as were followed where I have worked. Departments work out goals for the next fiscal year, often following centrally issued projections about cost levels and so on. These goals then travel up through the organization for consideration and evaluation. During their travels, the goals are generally increased. They then roam back to their point of origin, where, in their changed state, they become with varying success embedded or anchored.

Typically, traditional companies construct a future based on the past. The future goal is calculated by applying some plausible growth factor to prior performance. As these goals are established, detailed plans of how to reach them are formulated; the road to the goals is staked out. The operations of the company then amounts to following this staked-out road, and it is the task of the various managers to see that this is done. Managers also must give periodic reports to supervisors about the status of the advance along this road. The supervisors make sure the plan is followed and then report to their immediate superiors for verification. So it goes up through the entire organization.

From this perspective, one could say that the operation of a traditional company consists, on one hand, of setting goals and establishing a plan of action for reaching those goals and, on the other, of unfailingly following those established plans. Not surprisingly, those activities seem rather lifeless.

We Cannot Predict the Future

This way of conducting business not only is lifeless but also could jeopardize the future of a company. The future can no longer be predicted by projecting from the past. Company development no longer has that strongly linear and rather quiet course on which we earlier could depend. Today, development has a totally different course. It is rapid, very rapid, and it is irregular.

The future is not foreseeable. We cannot see even the nearest future with any accuracy. Goals can be set at the beginning of the fiscal year, realistic goals based upon prevailing conditions. But at the end of the year, so much may have changed that goals are no longer meaningful and could even be inconsistent with the needs of the business.

"But," someone may object, "we do observe the changes taking place around us, and we do adjust to them." I argue that that is not the case. Here lies the cardinal point: By setting goals we bind ourselves. We make up a plan to reach the goal and direct our activities accordingly. We walk as narrow and straight a road as possible toward the goal. Our fixation on the plan and the goal acts as blinders. We walk—as an old friend of mine expressed it— "in a tunnel." We have no ability to "catch the moment in its flight." We take no notice of what is happening on the side of the road. Openings, opportunities and signals could present themselves and not be noticed. And if we do notice them, we do not have time for them because they are interruptions and deviations from the established plan.

Everyone can recall occasions when a thought emerged or an unexpected proposition was presented, and our reaction was something like this: "That seems interesting. We really should look into this further, but it is not in line with what we are concentrating on right now. In any case we have to take care of more urgent matters, so right now there is no time." Then, when we eventually find or give ourselves time, we discover that conditions changed and the opportunity passed us by. It could have been a business idea, it could have been a meeting, a journey, a question that could have been answered. The missed opportunity could have given us new knowledge or new insights and could have made a contribution, not only to our personal development but also to the company for which we worked. It could have been a signal telling us that we were walking in the wrong direction.

Thus, to set goals and to work toward goals can be impediments to development. Furthermore, the realization of set goals does not necessarily give us anything, for it is not by reaching a set goal that we learn something. It is what we encounter along the way that gives us knowledge. There is profound wisdom in the ancient Eastern saying: "The road is the goal."

Business Without Goals?

Can we conduct business without goals? Can we conduct business without planning? I not only believe it is possible, but also I believe it is becoming a necessity.

The new company is not kept together by goals and plans. Instead, the "cement" in the new company is a vision that is shared by all. To reach this joint vision is the most important task of a company, because everything hinges on this vision. This vision is the foundation of the company, and it is the quest for this vision that deserves much time, much power and much energy.

Visions

What are visions? What is the difference between goals and visions? The answer is this: we *set* goals, but we *have* visions. The difference is subtle but of fundamental importance.

Let me explain by giving some examples. First, a personal one:

In the Introduction I told you some of my story. I described how I—without any deeper reflections about my life purpose—set up professional goals for my life. I described that I had reached those goals relatively early in my life and thereafter spent my time protecting what I had achieved and trying to find ways to climb even further. I described my awakening and my feelings of emptiness and meaninglessness. I described my grief, my anger. I described the pain, the searing pain that filled me. I described my longing.

Out of these feelings, out of this pain and longing, a vision was born. The vision was to live instead of to survive, to regard life as one big, exciting adventure, to wake up every morning curious about what that day will bring and to use my resources, knowledge and experiences to contribute, with inner engagement, to what I feel is meaningful.

Without going into detail, I can say that I am living a life that, compared with how it used to be, is exciting, eventful and filled with joy and lust for life. And above all: I feel my life has meaning.

I will offer another example, one from the world of politics, which mirrors, to some extent, a reverse development. In Chapter 4, "The New Thought," I described the miserable state that prevailed for the majority of the Swedish population at the turn of the century and how a vision of a new society was born out of the pain and the anger caused by those conditions. I also discussed how a number of high-spirited people succeeded in an astonishingly short time to totally reshape Swedish society. Finally, I described how, when the vision was well fulfilled, Sweden automatically continued on the same old road and ended up going downhill. There was no longer any vision.

Now the vision had been replaced by goals. The goals were (and still seems to be) to protect what had been achieved and to survive, that is, for the government to remain in power.

Before the vision was fulfilled, political power had been the means of realizing the vision. Now that there is no longer a vision, power has become an end in itself. As a consequence, the government and the people tend to think ahead only in periods of three years—the amount of time between elections. Economic policies are designed to be short term and to have immediate appeal to the voters. This type of planning takes place even though we all understand that these policies, in the long run, will bring us to catastrophe.

The employment situation is one example of planning for the short term in a way that is attractive to voters. In Sweden, as in most countries, the yardstick for measuring the success of the politics being conducted is the employment rate and, therefore, is of decisive importance to the voters in elections. To ensure high levels of employment, practically any method is accepted, be it the ravaging of nature, the exporting of weapons from "a peace-loving country" or, in recent years, a new polarization of the poor and the rich.

The same is true for the U.S. In fact, as I reviewed the material in this book prior to its being published here, I found that despite the different political and economic histories, the similarities between the current situations in Sweden and the U.S. are striking. Isn't it true that both countries were once carried by a vision? Isn't it true that power was only the means of realizing this vision, not an end in itself? Isn't it true that there is no longer an all-embracing vision, that the vision has been replaced by goals (More of the Same) and that power has become an end in itself? Isn't it true that the primary goal of political establishments is to remain in power or to acquire more power? Isn't it true that, as a consequence, the perspectives of both countries have become short sighted, focused only on the years between elections? Isn't it true that the economic policies are designed to be short term, to have an immediate appeal to the voters? U.S. politics may not be as strongly focused on full employment as is Sweden's, but isn't it true that the employment rate is considered a major yardstick of political success and, consequently, that maintaining a high employment rate is given a higher, short-sighted priority over more important, long-term priorities such as the preservation of nature?

To me, the similarities are indeed striking but not amazing, for though the histories may differ, the basic thinking—in terms of external growth and external power—in the two countries (and in all the Western world, for that matter) has been the same. Further, we are now witnessing in both countries how the old system is about to outgrow itself—how the soil is being prepared for a new vision to be born.

A final example of vision is from the business world: Öystein Skalleberg is an exceptional entrepreneur who runs an exceptional company, Skaltek AB, in Kungsängen, outside Stockholm. Skalleberg started his business career as a designer of wire machines employed by some of the large companies in the business. As he expressed it, the environment he worked in was characterized by lack of openness, poor information for the employees, dishonesty, manipulation, competition among individuals in the companies, fast money and a lack of keenness for new ideas. He recalled, "I wanted to go for quality. The owners wanted to make fast money. I wanted to develop and grow, but the lack of confidence, trust and honest openness killed my pleasure of working."

Out of this was born a vision to create a different kind of company. Skaltek AB started its operations in 1972 in a small basement shop outside Stockholm, designing, manufacturing and marketing packaging machines for the wire industry. The company now is located in a modern building in an industrial area of Kungsängen. It has about ninety employees and an annual net revenue equivalent to U.S. $17-18 million. About ninety-five percent of production is exported to some forty countries. There are branch companies in Germany and in the U.S. The company's motto is Simplicity and Quality—Security; the basic philosophy is that the capacity of the human being is matchless as long as the milieu is right.

At Skaltek no hierarchy or titles exist. Openness is total. Everyone in the company has access to all information. Each morning the entire staff meets for discussions and exchanges information about the volume of orders, the cash situation and similar matters. Staff members are not called employees, but rather responsible persons. All are—and perceive themselves to be—personally responsible. Control, as such, does not exist, not even quality control. On each packaging machine is a label on which is written "Quality—Security. I am responsible," with the signature of the person who has done the respective work. If there are any questions about the work later in the production chain, one doesn't turn to a foreman or a supervisor, but directly to the one responsible.

The company does not have a special sales force. The machines are designed and marketed through direct contacts between the customer and Skaltek's constructors and designers. Skaltek does not sell, but offers a solution to the potential customer's problem. The service agreement, normally part of an equipment purchase, does not exist. Instead, continuous follow-up inspections are provided for each delivered machine without the customer calling for service.

The company is focused on a vision of development, quality and service, not on profit. Nevertheless, at the time of this writing (winter 1992) Skaltek has a debt to equity ratio of one and a net profit level of about twenty percent of sales.

The vision of a different company, based on the thought that responsibility, confidence, trust, simplicity and quality create a milieu in which people's capacities and creativity can thrive, has resulted in a flourishing, living company in constant development.

As I hope has become clear by these examples, vision originates and emanates from a feeling. It is a manifestation of some longing: for a life with outer and inner harmony; for a fair society; for a company focused on development, quality and service instead of on profitability. In other words, a vision expresses an inner desire for something we wish to see realized.

A vision has no specific form. It is abstract, not measurable in terms of time and quantity, and it gives a direction. It has life, is constantly moving and growing during the course of the journey. There is no prescribed method of realizing a vision; a vision realizes itself. It attracts to itself the means of its own realization, thereby causing our actions to become focused in a certain direction. To a large extent it is an unconscious process experienced as "things just come to me."

A goal, by contrast, is not an expression of an inner desire. It lies outside ourselves and is not related to any specific meaning. For instance, I can imagine that those leaders of the Swedish labor movement old enough to have been active when the movement was carried by a vision, now find their work fairly meaningless compared to what it was like in earlier times. I can imagine that had Öystein Skalleberg been motivated by goals (for his company to grow in a planned way, to reach a certain level of profit and, for himself, to become a rich man), he would not feel that his work had been particularly meaningful even if he had reached the goals. I know that reaching set career goals was not particularly meaningful to me.

A vision emerges from a feeling; a goal is the result of logical thought. A goal is often the result of calculation or other analytical processes. It is brought about mechanically and is concrete- and time-bound. A goal is static; it does not change itself, but could, after further analytical processes, be the object of change. The goal has no life of its own.

A vision, on the other hand, is moving. It is in continuous development and growth. It has life.

Combining Goals and Visions

Could goals and visions be combined? Are not goals indispensable as stepping stones, even if we are being carried by a vision?

If you are being carried by a vision—a vision of creating a new company, for instance—your actions are steered in a certain direction; you intuitively see what is needed to be done at each moment to keep moving toward the realization of the vision, and you act accordingly. In acting accordingly, you are likely to take the organizational and planning steps necessary to achieve this realization. So, even an enterprise being directed by a vision has elements of goals and planning. There is an essential difference, though, between these goals and plans and those discussed earlier. These goals do not steer the action. These goals are not ends in themselves but the means to realize a vision. They are stepping stones. These goals and plans do not bind and blind us, because the vision within us ensures that our focus is beyond the goals.

The Vision Must Be Communicated

Earlier in this chapter, I somewhat boldly stated that everything hinges on vision and that finding the vision and keeping it alive is by far the most important business of a company. I hope the reader now sees that this was not an overstatement.

However, it is not enough to have a vision. A vision held by only one person or a few people working in an enterprise often does not have sufficient strength. A vision must be communicated to all, must be seen by all. It needs to be shared by all involved in the enterprise to have real force. It takes only one person who does not share an otherwise joint vision to drain power from the vision. That person, although deserving of respect, should be induced to leave the organization to go where he or she will find his or her vision.

A vision is not a thing of the moment. One cannot annually sit down to "check the vision." A vision is something we live. It is a consistently ongoing and growing process. The more devotedly we live our visions, the sooner they are realized. An example is the societal development in Sweden from the first decades of this century to the middle of the 1960s. Those who created that development lived their vision and lived it devotedly.

CHAPTER *11*

About Products

Since the rise of industrialism, our societies have become more and more production oriented. It is no exaggeration to say that societies in industrially developed countries are controlled by production interests, the inherent ambition to keep production at the highest possible level.

For a long time we have been living in an economic system characterized by mass production and mass consumption. The underlying premise is the following:

Mass production, it is argued, is necessary to maintain a high material standard of living for the majority of people. Mass production, in its turn, requires mass consumption. Mass consumption requires mass distribution of purchasing power. Mass distribution of purchasing power requires as high an employment rate as possible. In many societies this requirement has resulted in full employment becoming an end unto itself.

It is in light of these facts that we should examine the priority granted to production in the old way of thinking. Production has been given priority over such issues as what is actually being produced and the societal costs of that production.

Producers, Consumers and Marketing

To keep the economic wheels spinning, products must be consumed rapidly and efficiently. But in our mechanical way of thinking, we made a division between the functions of manufacturing and consumption, between producers and consumers. The products and the manufacturing of products is one area. The potential customers—the market—is another. The market in the eyes of the producers is "out there."

To sell products, consumers (or "the market") need to be massaged, manipulated, attacked or preferably conquered. Consumers must be induced to buy. This activity is called marketing and is as important a part of a company's business as is production! Marketing can have different degrees of intensity. If it is really intense, it is called aggressive, which in this context is considered a positive epithet.

Marketing strategy does not come into the picture only when a product is sold. Although the worst of the "use-it-and-throw-it-away" era seems to be over, we do still see many examples of marketing strategies affecting the production stage before anything is produced. Planned obsolescence, for example, still continues as a way to ensure product turnover and to secure a future market. Car batteries, for instance, seem to be built only for about five years of use. Many car manufacturers seem to create their products to last no longer than ten years.

Another way of creating rapid product turnover is frequent style change. Perhaps the most refined examples of this activity are in the fashion and car industries and, during recent years, in the electronics industry. Typically, a gadget with three functions is developed, but in phase one the product is presented with only one function. When the market is saturated the product is "upgraded" and is presented with two functions, later with all three. But the full product was there all the time.

Yet another way of securing product turnover is to delay implementation of technical innovations that may be of immediate benefit to consumers, introducing the innovations only when it becomes desirable to stimulate sales.

Similarly, there are instances of companies purchasing and then simply scrapping inventions that could have lowered consumption by increasing the life of the product, simplifying its production, or lowering the purchase price or cost of its operation.

Lobbying

Marketing, in the sense of sustaining or creating markets, also occurs in the form of lobbying. This practice is much more common than we are inclined to believe. By lobbying, I refer to the efforts of producers to induce politicians to make decisions more favorable to the producers than they are to the consumers. In Sweden, as in many other countries, the most efficient political inducement is to cite the positive effects a decision may have on the employment rate. The potential of negatively affecting the employment rate is also an efficient lever for inducing politicians not to make, or at least to delay, decisions that benefit consumers at the expense of producers.

One of the more spectacular examples of the lobbyist form of marketing is the so-called Big Conspiracy, which took place in the 1940s in the Los Angeles area at the beginning of its tremendous growth. The region had a well-planned and efficient public transportation system of electric trolleys, the Red Cars, and plans existed to extend the rail system in tempo with population growth.

Then, General Motors, Firestone Tires and Standard Oil joined to induce politicians in the area to abandon the rail car system in favor of a public transportation system based on gasoline-powered buses running on tires. The conspirators then bought the existing system and junked or sold the electric cars to prevent the government from ever going back to the rail car system. Anyone who has visited the Los Angeles area is well aware of the devastating results of this lobbying.

Of course, this kind of large-scale lobbying is not unique to the U.S. It is an intrinsic element of economic systems in most parts of the world. "The Big Conspiracy," in fact, is currently being repeated in northern Europe with the so-called Scanlink: a road system connecting Oslo (Norway), Gothenburg (Sweden), Copenhagen (Denmark) and some parts of Finland. Behind this project is a lobbying group consisting of some sixty corporations from those countries. Volvo has one of the more active roles, presumably trying to secure a future market for its truck production division. (As far as can be judged, the alternative to Scanlink is the expansion of the existing railway system.)

A portion of this project is a huge motorway along the west coast of Sweden. At the time of this writing (winter 1992), it is close to completion. Even though it was strongly opposed by the inhabitants of the area, the Swedish government ignored the opposition and approved the project. It should be of no surprise that this approval was preceded by intense lobbying activity by Volvo management, who took yet another opportunity to play the "employment card."

The inhabitants of the region can see beyond a few job opportunities. They know this motorway will increase pollution in an already fragile area and will severely encroach upon nature. Production interests, however, were given priority over human interests.

Consumer Protection

The strong emphasis on mass production and the resultant need for mass disposal of goods has reached such a state that it is easy to see the need for consumer protection from the abuse of producers. In most countries, consumer organizations have been founded and new legislation to protect consumers is gradually being implemented.

The New Company Begins with the Human Being and Has Meaning

The starting point of the new company is radically different. And, therefore, its results are radically different. People, not production, are the central issue.

The primary purpose of the new company is not to make as high a profit as possible. Instead, the focus is on the personal development and growth of all those who work in the company. The company exists to serve its employees and not, as in the traditional company, the other way around. Business has a meaning superior to the production and sale of goods, which is reflected in the company's relationship to the market. The company is there to serve the market, not to exploit it.

The starting point is no longer production and the subsequent need to sell. The intent is no longer to induce consumption of the company's products. Instead, the starting point is the consumer's need for goods and services. The company provides what appears to be meaningful.

Producers don't tell consumers what they need; consumers tell producers how and with which products they can best be served. There emerges, if you will, a reverse marketing: consumers inducing producers. Producers and consumers join in creative cooperation to satisfy the need for goods and services. The earlier distinction between those who produce and those who consume dissolves. The very terms producers and consumers more or less disappear from our common parlance.

From the companies' perspectives, this development leads to considerable inner as well as outer changes. (On top of this, the companies will face major adjustments due to demand pattern changes. This will be discussed later in the chapter.) Companies, by redefining their basic purpose, now have an inward meaning: they exist to serve as platforms or arenas for personal development and growth. By placing the needs of people above the needs of production, companies have an outward meaning as well: to serve their clients.

Because the company has an inward as well as an outward meaning, it follows that work takes on inward and outward meaning, too. It becomes meaningful to produce goods serving humankind. It is not meaningful to produce goods that do not fill any need or desire and must therefore be fobbed off on buyers. Rather, that gives us a feeling of exploiting our fellow humans.

Sales and Marketing Functions Are Reconsidered

If we look upon the outer changes that result from the new relationship between companies and customers, we can anticipate the natural effects on sales and marketing functions. Many companies will already be reconsidering these functions (which stand between producers and buyers) because of the cost and because they now strive for closeness (as described in Chapter 9, "About Organization"). Now, because of the inverted relationship between companies and their customers, the very needs for these functions will decrease or simply dissipate. In their place considerably expanded service functions will emerge.

Service with a New Focus

Service functions have aims other than those provided by the traditional company. The service commitments of the traditional company have little to do with care of the customer or the product. Services provided by the traditional company are primarily a marketing strategy and commonly come into play only after purchase. They are sales incentives that also provide a way for the company to capture as big a part as possible of the so-called after-market. The after-market, consisting of sales of spare parts and repair service, is responsible for an important portion of many companies' revenues and is, therefore, often the subject of sophisticated marketing gimmicks, such as extended service contracts, service insurance and the like.

In the new company, service functions are an expression of the company's care of and concern for both the customer and the product. These functions ensure that customers get exactly the products that best suit their needs. They also exist to ensure that products will be used in the best possible manner. Therefore, these functions of the new company come into play before purchase, with information and advice about product use, the suitability of the product for customers' needs, and other manufacturers' products that may better suit those needs.

In the new company, "after-service" is provided not only when called for by the customer but primarily on the initiative of the company, with continuous follow-up. The same care and concern with which the product was manufactured is also devoted to finding ways to follow the product during its lifetime. It is not done for the purpose of increasing sales or establishing an after-market, but for concern for the customer and for the product.

Which Products Are Demanded?

The interesting question now is, Which products will be manufactured when the interests of customers is given priority over the interests of producers? For which goods and services will we find a need?

Of course, I cannot give a detailed prognosis about needs other than my own. However, I don't think it is particularly difficult to envision some general trends based upon the characteristics of the new way of thinking now emerging.

Every human being is unique and has unique needs

Let us start with one of the mainstays of the new way of thinking: the acknowledgement that every human being is unique. This leads us away from the uniformity that characterizes so much of our lives today. We seek, assert and accept our individuality as well as the individuality of others. Our needs are determined on that basis instead of on external pressures. We no longer follow trends, common patterns, or the path considered suitable to our age or our position in society.

We dare to diverge from the norm and accept the divergences of others. We ask, "What is *my* need?", "What do *I* want?", "What suits *me?*"

The manifestation of individuality not only will result in changes to or elimination of the familiar mass buying trends, but also will lead to a demand for more individualized products. We can therefore assume that the demand for many standard products distributed in mass quantities will gradually decrease and will be replaced by a demand for products tailor-made to the individual customer's needs.

The Larger Perspective

In the new way of thinking, every human being is not only considered to be unique but is also understood to be a part of, or connected with, every other human being. In the new thinking, there is the awareness that everything—human beings as well as nature—constitutes a whole. We therefore apply an essentially larger perspective than our previously short-sighted and egotistic interests when determining our needs.

We are starting to realize that our preoccupation with rapid economic growth has led to over-consumption of human as well as natural resources. We are beginning to see through the illusion that economic growth is tantamount to progress. We are beginning to ask ourselves, "What can I do without?" rather than, "What do I want?" We are discovering that a great number of products are unnecessary. As this awareness grows, no organized campaign will be needed to bring about a radical change in consumption patterns.

When it comes to evaluating products, we begin to carefully weigh our personal needs against what is consumed in the production as well as in the use of that product. We will avoid as much as possible products manufactured under unacceptable human conditions, products that deplete natural resources, and products manufactured by methods that pollute or encroach upon nature. The same applies to product use that draws on and consumes the resources of our planet. The life expectancy of products will also be of decisive importance in determining product demand. Many positive changes will result from the application of such criteria.

To reiterate, these changes will not be the result of organized actions or campaigns, but, rather, an awareness that will grow with increasing intensity within individuals.

The Industrial Conversion from Productivity to Flexibility

Let us now consider what these developments entail for companies. It is easy to see that the growing demand for individualized or tailor-made products will necessitate big changes in production methods.

Today, mass production is considered to be the most efficient way to use people and machines. Much energy and creativity is devoted to the design of production assembly lines that describe in great detail each operation and the amount of time allowed for that operation. When the production layout is established, the ideal is to have the production running with as few mechanical or human disruptions as possible. The humans used are subservient to the overall production scheme. Control devices make sure that no deviations take place, and creative contributions are discouraged, if not altogether prevented.

With the transition to individual demand, it follows that the main emphasis of manufacturing departments will shift from mass productivity to flexibility, and companies that cannot meet the diversified demands of their customers will simply not have markets. Furthermore, flexible production methods will require and encourage creativity from those directly involved with production, thereby making work in those sectors more meaningful than before.

The introduction of increased flexibility into production facilities is not the only consequence of the transition to meeting individualized demand. Another result that is just as important—and in a way more interesting and exciting—will be the rise of many new, often smaller and perhaps only locally active companies that specialize in satisfying the needs of a limited circle of customers.

Reduced Production Volume

The most profound problems for our industries that result from the transition, however, will be brought forth by the lowering of the general consumption level. As large numbers of products become unnecessary or undesirable, production levels will be reduced. Many companies in operation today will be forced to radically change their products, develop more environment-friendly production methods, or curtail and in some cases close their operations. Those companies that quickly adjust not only to the changed patterns of consumption but also to human needs, will have the best chances of survival.

It is inevitable that a reduction in production volume will significantly affect employment levels, particularly when reduced volume is accompanied by further automation of production methods. We will be able to produce the goods needed and desired with significantly fewer people than are now employed in production areas. As is explained in the next chapter, "About Work," this is not as negative a development as we at first may be inclined to believe. Rather, it is important human progress. To fully appreciate the positive nature of this change, however, we must totally reevaluate the way we view work and its role in our society.

CHAPTER *12*

About Work

"The measure of a man's work is not what he has obtained from it, but what he has become of it."

*E*ven though this quotation (the author unfortunately unknown to me) specifically relates to work, it has bearing on life as a whole. In these words lies the existential core of the new thought. We do not exist to survive, but to live. We do not exist to obtain things—to make money, to gain position and power, to collect possessions and thereby prove our worth to ourselves and others; we exist to learn, to develop and to grow as human beings.

Life Is the Meaning

The meaning of life is life itself—the process of living—and not what we accumulate along the way. We must not look at life as a struggle lest it becomes one. We must embrace life and openly receive what comes to us, positive as well as negative, big as well as small. We can develop only by meeting challenges, problems, and difficulties and testing our capacity to deal with them. This is how we learn, and this is how we can reach our practically unlimited inner resources. This is how we become aware, perhaps with amazement but above all with joy, of the creativity we all posses. This is how we acquire experiences, insights, knowledge and, eventually, wisdom. And this is of benefit not only to ourselves as individuals but to the whole of humankind.

When it comes to work, the new way of thinking inevitably leads us to reconsider the role of work (and, along with it, the role of business). In this chapter I address the role of work from two perspectives: one starting from the individual and the other from society. Such a division could be questioned, and as we will see later, these perspectives are closely interrelated and begin at the same place: the human being. However, I think clarity will best be served by considering them separately.

The role of work viewed from the perspective of the individual is discussed in terms of its meaning for those performing the work, that is, the purpose of work. The role of work viewed from the perspective of society is discussed in terms of its contribution to society. Is work the only way we can contribute to our society and to our fellow humans?

The Purpose of Work

Let me summarize what was previously discussed about the purpose of work. A new way of thinking is developing naturally within humankind. It is a result of human evolution and not of any organized activity with religious or political overtones. The new thought grows of its own power, and it is growing rapidly. It is not something that can be stopped. Consequently, we would be wise to accept it and view it with great seriousness.

As a result of the new thought, many of us have begun to seek jobs that offer opportunities for inner, personal development rather than only material rewards. We no longer seek arenas for obtaining as much position, power and economic return as possible. We seek arenas that provide opportunities for our personal growth. Unconsciously and consciously, we have begun to give the purpose and the meaning of work a new definition, namely this:

> Work, as every other aspect of life, is a process, through which we acquire experiences and insights and grow inwardly. The production of goods and services and economic return for work, are by-products of this process.

It is in light of this new definition that we should view the alienation now emerging and spreading in our places of work. One symptom now observable anywhere in the industrialized world is the disturbingly high rate of absenteeism—physical and mental (we go to our jobs but are not particularly engaged in what we are doing there). In Sweden there are companies with absentee rates of up to forty percent. The absentee problem has become so severe that many companies have introduced what is called presence bonuses: a worker whose number of absentee days does not exceed a certain amount during a defined period of time is, on top of ordinary wages, entitled to a special premium.

Another symptom is the increasing tendency among young people to find ways of making a living other than working in traditional companies. People's ideas about the meaning of work simply do not correspond with companies' prevailing thoughts about the meaning of business. A research report, based on an inquiry made within the Swedish manufacturing industries and published in June 1989, caused headlines in the Swedish newspapers such as "The young are fleeing the industries." The report cited, among other things, the increasing difficulty in recruiting students to take industrial courses in high schools and colleges. It reported that the young have a very negative attitude towards industrial work in general. The tasks are perceived as meaningless, and many of those having industrial jobs are ashamed to tell people about their work. Communication with managers is not functional, and the opportunities of personal development are considered to be too few. Said one worker, "Many of my colleagues are proud of the fact that their children do not have industrial jobs."

As long as we adhere to the traditional definition of the meaning of business—that its primary purpose is to achieve the highest possible profit—the gap between people and companies will continue and increase at an ever-accelerating rate. This gap will result in, among other things, further deterioration of our psychological and physical well-being.

Therefore, to reach harmony between people and companies, it is necessary to redefine the meaning and purpose of business to the following:

> The primary purpose of a company is to serve as an arena for
> the personal development of those working in the company. The
> production of goods and services and the making of profits are
> by-products.

There are some serious and laudable efforts being made in many parts of the industrialized world to create better working conditions and stimulate work pleasure. Essentially, these efforts are directed toward improving the physical work environment, such as attractive buildings, interior decoration and the reshaping of work tasks. To some extent, efforts are also being made to include employees in the decision-making process. Even though these efforts to some extent are prompted by sincere caring for the people involved, the driving force behind these efforts is, nevertheless, concern for profits. By creating more pleasant working conditions and increasing work motivation, we could, it is argued, achieve higher productivity, higher quality, lower absenteeism and, with that, improved profitability.

But we don't achieve harmony among employees and companies this way. Harmony comes about only when the companies' ideas about the purpose of business are in line with the employees' ideas about the purpose of work. Only when companies and employees unite in purpose to form a whole within which companies serve the employees, only when employees perform work in order to get energy rather than lose it, does harmony exist. Then, and only then, work becomes an integrated part of our lives and not the major portion of the day when we cease to be ourselves just to make the money to live. In the new thought, the day is whole and not chopped up into work time, leisure time and sleep time.

The Role of Work in Society

In the beginning of our civilization, the role of work was confined to the survival of the individual, the family or the tribe. Over time, work became a more and more important societal affair. In most societies today, work (often called occupation) has become the overshadowing issue. The importance of work is linked with the perception (engraved on our minds over thousands of years) that people *shall* work, and that it is through work we achieve value as human beings. With this perception as a basis, the most important task of society has long been considered to be providing job opportunities to as many people as possible. Initially, this was probably done more out of care for the needs of the individual than for society. However, the idea that providing job opportunities is the most important task of society has led us into a more and more vicious circle.

To create job opportunities, we first concentrated on production and eventually on mass production. Then, to be able to sell the mass produced goods, we needed mass consumption. Mass consumption necessitated mass distribution of purchasing power. For this, we needed as many individuals as possible to be out there in salaried jobs, and the circle closes.

In this circle, the human aspects of work have been overshadowed by the societal, that is, the economic aspects, and the human beings have become prisoners on this treadmill. Like a hamster on a wheel, their role is to keep the wheel spinning: by productive work in mass production as well as by consumption—mass consumption—of the results of that work. Work is no longer there for the workers. The workers are there for the economy to spin.

In this scenario, being productive is no longer simply a virtue. It has become a requirement; it has gotten a more metallic clang. The perception of work has hardened. If we are not productive, we do not contribute to the development of society. Then, we have no value and become unnecessary.

Economic Growth—Yet Another Vicious Circle

There is another vicious circle enclosing and nurturing the one previously discussed. The course of this larger circle looks like this:

Products are sold in a competitive market. One important competitive factor is a product's price. Therefore, production costs must be kept to a minimum. In most cases, the cost of labor is the greatest part of the production cost. It is also the part that can be most easily controlled with the help of technological evolution: we can automate production. However, as the automation increases, the number of people needed for production decreases. Accordingly, to keep the first circle functioning in spite of reduced purchasing power due to fewer jobs, we have to compensate for this reduction. That we do by increasing production levels. Markets must then be found for the additional production. Markets require purchasing power. To ensure that purchasing power is sufficient to sustain the market, production costs must be kept low. Efforts to further lower production costs encourage more automation. Automation absorbs job opportunities and further lowers purchasing power. Again we have to compensate. And on it goes.

We call this process (increased production and increased consumption) economic growth. The underlying politics supporting this process we call economic politics, which, in its turn, is supported by another politics we call employment politics. Where is the human politics in all this?

It is difficult to see the driving force behind these processes. Has full employment, or at least as high an employment rate as possible, become an end in itself? Is the driving force economic growth? Is it, perhaps, both? Is the employment rate a reflection of economic well-being and, as such, an indication of the competence of the government in office? Or, has being in office—having political power—become an end in itself?

Although these questions are worth asking, they are not directed at the real issues. The overshadowing fact is that the human being is no longer part of the game; our economic system lies outside human beings and has made us its prisoners.

It is tragic that the developing countries are using this model as a goal for their development. It is remarkable that we have brought this about at all. Undoubtedly, there is much to what an old friend of mine says: "Man's worst enemy is man himself."

We Start Seeing but Our Thoughts about Work Impede the Change of Course

In our fervor to keep the wheels spinning, in our fervor over growth, we have become blind (or have consciously closed our eyes) to the fact that for the last twenty-five years or so this growth has been possible only by ruthlessly exploiting our human and natural resources. When we in the industrialized countries have been forced to cut down on the ruthless exploitation of our own people, we have taken advantage of the precarious economic situations of developing countries—situations for which we are largely responsible—and simply moved the exploitation there.

Growth has not improved or augmented anything. It has drained, consumed and devoured, and continues to do so.

Over the years, many people have called attention to this state of affairs. They have not been heard. Instead, they have often been ridiculed as being "flaky eco-freaks," "brown-ricers," "voluntary primitives" and so on. When their protests have become a little too drastic and evident, they have been forcibly silenced. Even though these people have been largely ignored, I believe they have greatly influenced our unconscious awareness that the road is leading in the wrong direction. Their efforts have enabled us to see how our actions are creating physical and mental problems for great numbers of people and one environmental catastrophe after the next.

Although this has now become clear to many of us, we resist making the radical changes that are becoming more and more necessary. What is most responsible for this resistance is our inherent way of looking upon work. Yes, we say to ourselves, a radical change of course is necessary. But how could we make this change and still maintain or improve present employment levels?

Economically, as we continue our discussion with ourselves, it may be possible to make it in our society (for instance, with changed ways of income distribution) even with high unemployment levels. But will we make it psychologically? Socially? Isn't it devastating to most people to be idle? After all, human beings need occupation and we do derive our self-esteem and personal identity from work. Unemployment, accordingly, is perceived by most people to be a personal catastrophe because they think they will feel unnecessary if they are unemployed.

Yes, such psychosocial problems could be unsurmountable. As I see it, there is only one way to remove these problems, and that is to fundamentally—deep down in the farthest nooks of our souls—change our thoughts about work.

The Issue Involves More Than the Reduction of Job Opportunities Caused by Stopping Growth

Before clearly identifying these changes in our thoughts about work, we must clarify the whole scope of the issue. It is not limited to the decline of job opportunities caused by halting economic growth. A declining level of consumption is another contributing factor.

Furthermore, technological evolution will continue, enabling further automation of the production process. This evolution should not be avoided just to keep greater numbers of people employed. It is not particularly meaningful to perform tasks that could be executed just as well as or even better by machines or by robots.

In this context, we should also pay attention to the growing *under*employment. Educational programs have produced many young people who cannot find work commensurate with the their educational level. Well-educated blue-collar and white-collar workers find that they have to accept routine work or at least work that does not require an education. Many people with some higher education are disappointed to find that many career opportunities once available to educated individuals no longer exist.

Considering the prevailing perception of work, under- employment is probably more responsible for the increasing alienation of workers than previously imagined. The problem of underemployment can only be expected to become more severe as standards of education remain high, production volume drops and automation spreads.

Technical Solutions
Do Not Remove Psychosocial Problems

To sum up, we are facing a situation in which the goods and services required by our societies can be produced by only a small fraction of the potential work force. Additionally, many who are working will be underemployed. General debate has brought forward several suggestions regarding how to technically meet this situation. These suggestions have included reduced working hours (shorter working days, longer vacations, sabbaticals, early retirements and so on). They have included ideas about government grants to the unemployed for studies or "just for thinking." It has been suggested that work be limited to a certain period of our lives, after which we would be salaried by the government and allowed to dispose of our time as we thought best, and so on.

I favor a solution in which we sandwich periods of work between periods of unrestricted free time.

However, I shall not address technical solutions here. No technical solution could possibly remove the psychosocial problems arising from so-called high unemployment or mass unemployment. We have to change our way of thinking about the role of work in our societies. We have to change our inherited and rigid values relating to work. We need to see to it that expressions such as "employment," "unemployment," "job opportunities" and the like disappear from our parlance.

Let us acquaint ourselves with what happens to a person in our present value system who becomes unemployed. I have been without "proper" employment after periods of intense and absorbing work. Thus, I speak from my experience.

As I see it, the psychosocial problems resulting from unemployment have to do with meaning. It is not that we have necessarily accepted the old thoughts about work as the meaning of life. It is more likely that we have grabbed hold of work as a means of slipping away from the existential questions; to be occupied by work, to have an assignment, simply fills a vacuum.

However, it goes further than that. Work is used as a means of running away from ourselves and of avoiding our feelings. The old thought's close alliance with logical processes has made us afraid of our feelings. We are not just afraid of showing them; we are afraid of having them at all. Work has become one of the drugs we use to deaden and block the emotional aspect within us. For many of us—men as well as women—this has gone so far that we cannot enjoy our leisure time. We cannot relax. In fact, in many cases we dare not relax lest our emotions are given a chance to pop up. We even bring work into our homes either on paper or in our heads. When not working, we engage ourselves in organized activities of different kinds. We kill time in front of the television and so on.

In this light, it is easy to see that unemployment is a personal, psychological and emotional catastrophe for most individuals, regardless of the economic consequences. It is not only that we lose the self-esteem and sense of self-identity that were supplied by having a job; but also the positive identity work has given us is replaced by the negative identity, the stigma, of being unemployed. It is not only that we feel pressure to do our share and be a contributing member of society that we simply feel unnecessary, but also we can easily end up feeling empty and meaningless and having lost a tool to shield ourselves from our emotions.

Unemployment is one of the most personally destructive situations a person can face. It is not because unemployment is inherently negative; it is the result of our beliefs, our thinking, about the nature and value of work.

We Must Change Our Thought About Work

To successfully make the transition from production-oriented to people-oriented economies without severe psychosocial disturbances, we must change our evaluation of work. This reevaluation is brought about by applying the new thought.

In the new thought, life is seen as a developmental process in which we grow as human beings. Life has no specific goal beyond the process itself. The process—life itself, if you want—is the meaning, not the possessions, position and fame gathered along the way.

Work, then, is one aspect of life. It is one way of learning and acquiring new experiences and insights, but it is by no means the only way. All aspects of life give us arenas for our development.

Our family life does. So does time spent with others, regardless of the context. Helping others does, as does receiving help from others. A ride in the car does. A walk by yourself in the forest does. Studying does, not the kind of studying when we stuff other people's knowledge into ourselves, but studies whereby through questioning and contemplation we develop new thoughts and ideas. Research work does. Tranquil fishing does, with nature and the coming and going of thoughts and feelings as the only company. Writing a book does (whether or not it is published). All experiences can provide meaningful arenas if we openly receive life, participate in its conflicts and observe what it reveals to us.

No standards of behavior apply, whether promulgated by the authorities or developed from peer valuations. Each of us must determine what is best for ourselves, for each situation is unique.

In a society in which the focus is human development rather than production, work has no greater worth than any other aspect of life. But, we may ask, isn't the one who works contributing more to society than the one who just walks around thinking? After all, the former's activities are of benefit to all in that they produce goods and services needed or desired by others and the latter's is of personal benefit only.

I do not see it that way. One of the cornerstones of the new thought is that everything is interrelated. Every part of what we call creation is interconnected with every other part. Each human being is not only unique but is also a part of every other human being. Therefore, each additional growth, each new insight, that I as an individual acquire contributes to the insight of every other individual, regardless of whether the insight is attributable to me or has a broader application. With every insight gained, the total knowledge of humankind expands yet another step. The paradox, then, is that the more I invest in myself and my own development by putting myself in the center, letting things come to me, accepting challenges and so on, the more I contribute to my fellow human beings.

To Sum Up

Work is not worth more than any other aspect of our existence. One who works does not contribute more than one who has chosen some other arena for personal growth. With this change in our view of the role of work, we can eliminate concepts such as employment, unemployment and the like from our parlance. With this shift we can also eliminate the perception that the distribution of income necessarily should be linked to work.

Finally, we have to learn to accept that we have within us an emotional aspect that is as strong as our logical aspect. If we dampen or block our emotions, they will emerge in destructive ways. If we give them recognition and expression, they will become constructive parts of our lives. It is in the balance between feeling and logic that we reach inner harmony.

CHAPTER 13

About Profits

I hope it is clear that the fundamental difference between the traditional and the new company is that the former is results oriented while the latter is process oriented. This difference is reflected in how these types of companies view and use profits.

Traditional Companies Are Being Drained

In the traditional company, profit is the reason for being in business. It is then only natural that the profits are primarily used to enable future profits to be as great as possible. In the new company, the process is the purpose; the profits are a by-product. Therefore, in the new company it is natural that profits are used primarily to support the process. The traditional company uses its profits to achieve outer growth; the new company uses profits to achieve inner growth.

The traditional company is drained of the energy it generates. In the new company, the energy is circulated.

Let us examine the traditional company. To begin with, the mechanical way of looking at things (a characteristic of the old thought) fragments the wholeness of a company. We see this in organizational methods like establishing different departments (a common pattern is, for instance, to segment design, production and marketing-sales functions from one another) and different product lines. We see it in the division of workers (hourly salaried blue-collar workers, on the one hand, and monthly salaried white-collar workers on the other). We see it in the hierarchical system.

This mechanistic thinking is also applied to such abstract matters as generating and distributing profit. After the profit is generated, when the workers of the company have "done their part" and "gotten their share," the profit is detached from its source (the process) and treated as something separate. It becomes a numerical figure in an abstract arena; it becomes an entity with a life of its own.

I think this is the root of traditional companies' predisposition to use profits for outer expansion instead of for inner growth, thereby draining energy from the process that generated that profit. The detachment of profit from its source removes any restraints on the ambitions for external growth inherent in the old thought's maxim "bigger is better." The potential for expansion and growth is regarded as being more important than the health of the process that generates the profit.

There are many justifications presented for this position. It is necessary to diversify to spread the risk. It is important to control as many links as possible in the production chain by vertical or horizontal integration. A company must aim at large-scale advantages. A company needs to buy market share and preserve, if not improve, a competitive edge.

Regardless of what is stated, any such reason has as its source the same maxim, "bigger is better." "Bigger" bestows power and influence. "Bigger" is prestigious. A management that expands into new business areas by milking a profitable company is seen as dynamic. In management literature and at business schools, strategies and techniques of profit diversion are actually taught. Companies that are candidates for such plundering are referred to as "cash cows." On the other hand, a management that is content with taking good care of the original company is often disparagingly referred to as "conservative."

More and more companies are now realizing that this is not a particularly successful policy. Draining profits from the organization that generates them devitalizes that organization and eventually kills it.

There are many examples, both in Europe and in the U.S., of this practice. Once-vital companies are forced to cut back or close, not because of structural changes in the surrounding world, but because the energy has been drained from them. We will probably continue to see more examples of this development.

Before examining the new company, allow me these observations about detaching profit from its source. Isn't this practice the nucleus of our rampant and devastating speculation economy? Isn't this the reason that money—energy originally generated by humans—has become our largest commodity that we buy, sell, loan and borrow? I will come back to the issue of our speculation economy in Chapter 15, "About the World Economy."

The New Companies Are Being Nourished

The new company is process oriented. Its raison d'être is to provide people in the company with the best possible conditions for developing their creativity, acquiring experiences and insights, and increasing their knowledge.

The new company is not separated into parts; it is perceived as and operates as a whole. The new company is a system in which the process and the resulting profits are not separated; the process does not end with obtaining profit because profit is not the purpose of the process. The new company emulates nature; it is a system in which energy (profit) is recirculated.

The purpose of keeping profits within the company is to nourish the process, that is, to nourish the personal development of the people in the company. The fact that the energy is actually circulated is a cardinal point. One can vary the course of the energy flow as needed, including funding investments for the future development of the process. But the accumulation of profits to increase the value of the company—as is often the case in the traditional company—lies outside the idea of the new company. Such "money piles" are nothing but locked-up dead energy that serves no function.

Outer expansion is not excluded for the new company. Such expansion is not, however, an end in itself. It is either a by-product of the inner growth or something that serves to broaden the base for the inner growth.

CHAPTER *14*

About Ownership

*I*n order for the new company to adhere to the principles previously discussed and to be a workable business, current forms of ownership must be reconsidered. Without a suitable owner environment, the new company will not achieve its
full potential. Before exploring alternative ownership models,
let us first review some of the main points from the preceding
chapter.

- The practically unlimited inner resources of the human
  being are, beyond comparison, our largest resource. We
  are becoming more and more aware of these resources;
  our greatest challenge is to discover and develop them.
  It is by increasing creativity that true growth is
  achieved.

- The old thought, with its logical materialistic outlook
  and obsession with outer growth, confines human
  resources. It is paradoxical that the more our awareness
  of the human being's tremendous potential grows, the
  more we deny ourselves the ability to develop it. We

111

protect ourselves from the old thought, which wants to exploit our inherent creativity by using it for yet more outer growth. Such growth we find meaningless.

- As we begin searching for a deeper meaning, a new thought emerges. This new thought is not a revolt against the old thought; it naturally evolves from it. One of the cornerstones of new thought is that as we reach into and develop our inner resources; we grow as human beings. We change our focus from outer to inner growth.

- Applied to business, the new thought changes our view of work. We see that the primary purpose of work is to offer opportunities for personal and human growth. All else, including economic return, is secondary.

- Furthermore, the new thought leads to a changed understanding of business. The primary purpose of a company is to serve as an arena or platform for the personal development of its employees. All else, including profitability and expansion, is secondary.

- This complete change of thought about work and business encourages radical changes in the way in which we organize our companies. The purpose of organizational forms is no longer to achieve the highest possible efficiency, productivity and profitability, but to create the best possible conditions for the development of human creativity.

- The cornerstones of the new organizational forms are closeness, openness and flexibility. However, the most revolutionary concept is the absence of a power-based hierarchy. In the new company power is not concentrated anywhere; it is distributed everywhere.

Which Ownership Form Best Fits into the New Picture?

Let us consider which form of ownership best suits the new company. We are looking for a form of ownership in which power elements have, for the most part, been eliminated. We are looking for a form of ownership with as few external claims on the company as possible. We are looking for a form of ownership that reflects our yearning for a relationship between companies and employees other than the mechanical relationship characteristic of the traditional companies. We are looking for a form of ownership that makes us feel that we belong. We seek an ownership model that creates the best possible conditions for our personal development.

None of the prevailing ownership models currently in use is suitable for the new company. For the sake of simplicity, we can refer to them as the socialistic and the capitalistic models. Both models provide ways of expressing power. Both imply that certain people, solely by virtue of ownership, position or both can make decisions that directly or indirectly affect other human beings without seeking their advice or consent. Furthermore, in the socialistic model, an institution, the State, assumes ownership. In the capitalistic model, ownership also has been assumed for the most part by institutions: large corporations (often with interlocking ownerships and directorates), insurance companies, banks and other financial institutions, or funds of various kinds.

Thus, the two models are not only methods of expressing power, but they also imply that ownership and power do not rest with human beings at all but with impersonal, technical apparatuses. This is completely true of the socialistic model and largely true of the capitalistic model. Opportunities for contact between the owners and the employees of the companies do not exist, for the most part. In all likelihood, the involvement of the owners of companies is largely mechanical, and their interests are confined to either the welfare of the State or to productivity and profitability.

The apparatuses have lives apart from the human beings and as owners they do not take part in the day-to-day lives of the companies they own and control. They are what we usually call absentee owners. Apparatuses naturally have no interest in human beings other than as tools for the fulfillment of their interests. The interests of the apparatuses take precedence over everything else. These apparatuses constitute the sectors of our societies that are furthest removed from nature. Apparatuses have no feelings and are not predisposed to care; they express concern for nature only when forced to do so.

Thus, institutional ownership simply does not correspond with the thought that a company's primary purpose is to serve as a platform or arena for the personal development of its employees. In that respect, I do not see any dissimilarity between State and private institutional ownership.

Companies owned by individuals (generally called family companies) more closely correspond with the new thought. In these companies, the owners are not absentee; they are directly involved in the operation of the company. Yet, no matter how much the owner(s) may embrace the new way of thinking, it is inevitable that this form of ownership also contains elements of power concentration and, therefore, does not fit into the new picture.

Ownership By the Employees

I cannot see any ownership model that better corresponds to the new way of thinking than ownership by those who are employed by the company. I refer to direct employee ownership, not the indirect ownership claimed to exist in socialistic countries. I also refer to ownership, by and large, equivalent among the employees. In this ownership model, no individual or group of individuals has more power or influence than another. Neither are there any absentee owners.

This ownership model implies that not only is there no concentration of power, but also there are no external claims on the company. There are no outside interests draining energy from the company and the developmental process that needs that energy. In this ownership model, the employees and the company form a whole. The employees are the company. The companies are living entities, and the human creativity, previously suffocated, can blossom.

To avoid any misunderstanding, I must emphasize that this ownership model has as its sole purpose the creation of the best possible conditions for the development of human resources. It is not concerned with providing employees an opportunity to increase their personal wealth by increasing the value of the company. True, it is presumed that the new company will, if only as a by-product, generate profits and plow any excess back into the company. However, the purpose of keeping profits within the company is not to accumulate wealth, but to supply the energy necessary for the developmental process to continue and to improve. This ownership model implies that the value of the shares should be kept reasonably stable; too big an increase in the value could obstruct the transfer of the shares that is assumed to occur when personnel changes take place.

As an example of employee ownership, let me describe the system practiced for more than twenty years by Bookpeople, a wholesale book distribution company in Oakland, California. Founded in 1968, Bookpeople was bought out from the original owners by its employees in 1971. At the time, the company had twenty employees and generated gross sales of $1.8 million. At the time of this writing the company has some eighty employees, all shareholders, and gross sales exceeding $20 million.

In 1971 the employees, dedicated to finding an alternative to standard proprietorship, invented and implemented a system whereby ownership could be shared equally by all current workers. In essence the system works like this: Each full-time and regular part-time employee owns (and has to own) a block of 50 shares. No one can buy additional shares, nor can any non-employee buy shares. Each block of 50 shares has a fixed value of $500. Each new employee is on probation for six months. If after probation there is mutual consent, the worker is no longer on probation and becomes a shareholder. He or she then gets a special raise, or "shareholder increase," of $100 per month and can choose either to pay the $500 in full or to pay by paycheck deductions for a period not exceeding twelve months. Employment can be terminated, voluntary or involuntary (as in any other company) because of serious infraction of company rules, unsatisfactory performance and so on. When the employee leaves the company, the shares are sold back to the company at the fixed value.

As stated in Bookpeople's bylaws, the owners "delegate to company's Board of Directors the responsibility and authority for governing the company on owners' behalf." The board consists of five members chosen annually by the shareholders. Each shareholder has 250 votes to be distributed in any way desired among candidates. Only employees can serve on the board and each employee/shareholder (regardless of position or time spent with the company) is eligible. The main responsibilities of the board are to set company policies and to appoint company officers and department heads.

Bookpeople's salaries are primarily linked to years spent with the company, rather than to position. Only in some rare occasions when there has been a need to hire someone from the outside with special qualifications have exceptions been made. Each year the board decides how much of the profit should be retained within the company "to promote the financial solvency of the corporation in order to provide for the need and general welfare of [our] shareholder/employees." The balance is used for an equally shared bonus to the employees. In addition, there usually is a small dividend distributed to the employees.

As said, this rather simple and uncomplicated system has worked for more than twenty years, obviously to the satisfaction of all involved.

Offers of Shares or Convertibles—a Step on the Road?

Someone may suggest that the practice, especially by large corporations, of giving employees the opportunity to buy shares (normally stocks or convertibles) in "their" companies may be a step in the direction toward the new ownership model. (A convertible is in essence a loan to the company that at a fixed date by the lender's choice should be either paid back or converted into shares of the company at a rate settled when the convertibles were issued.)

Is this practice perhaps a sign of progressive thinking? As far as I can determine, this practice is nothing but another expression of the old thought's preoccupation with materialism and profitability. This "offer" is only a desperate attempt at self-preservation. The employees are still regarded as mere tools for achieving profitability and expansion. By luring the employees with promises of increased wealth, they can be induced to work hard, be productive and be loyal to the company in the face of growing alienation and displeasure. By using money as medicine, companies are attempting to cure the symptoms while ignoring the disease.

A case is Saab's program, offered in the summer of 1988, that allowed employees to acquire convertibles in the company. A news article in the Stockholm daily, the *Dagens Nyheter* (Aug. 14, 1988), quoted Saab's then executive vice president, Kai Hammerich: "Our hope is that the individual worker down at the assembly line now will work more efficiently and will put himself on the sick list less often. That is the idea behind convertibles."

Furthermore, the impression of these offers is not improved by the fact that the programs are often discriminatory; There are examples of top managers being given (or giving themselves?) the opportunity to acquire blocks of stock many times larger than the blocks offered to those further down in the hierarchy. I think these offers are nothing more than attempts to assuage the dissatisfaction of lower-echelon workers while adding to the potential wealth of upper-echelon management.

Consequently, I cannot see that this more and more common practice of giving employees the opportunity to "buy" into their companies is an expression of new thinking. It accomplishes nothing more than compounding the captivity of human beings by the economic system.

Some national unions have also criticized this scheme. However, I believe this criticism is less motivated by concern for the workers than by concern for the union organizations themselves. The unions fear that these plans blur the distinction between employer and employee, thereby weakening the unions' hold over its members. It is this hold that allows the unions to maintain their power.

A New Ownership Model Emerges Naturally

How, then, could this change of ownership model come about? Isn't it a prerequisite for the current economic system to collapse and a new system to be built upon the ruins? Could the necessary changes take place within the present system?

I believe there are many indications that our present economic system is on its way to collapse (an issue I discuss in the next chapter). However, I do not think collapse is a prerequisite for implementation of or even rapid transition into the model here described.

Let me again remind the reader that the evolution now taking place is not the result of efforts by an organized political movement. There is no movement, and the progress of the evolution is not organized. Rather, it is a consequence of a change—a rising and stretching—of human consciousness. It is a natural, self-perpetuating evolution, not a revolt. Therefore, implementation of the new ownership model does not include coercive measures such as confiscation, which, historically, has never resulted in anything positive.

No, the new ownership model emerges naturally and is supported by the new way of thinking. It is likely that this model is being implemented within existing, smaller companies and especially within companies now being created. (I think a common example is the entrepreneur or visionary who starts a company as sole owner and, after the company has become established and has attracted the right participants, transfers ownership to the employees.) The smaller companies will serve as examples for the larger companies, which, if nothing else, will be astounded by the vitality and the creativity being developed in the new companies.

However, we will also see examples of companies (large corporations, especially) becoming more and more rigidly entrenched in the old thought, doing everything to maintain the old system and avoiding adoption of the new model. It would be a waste of time and energy to attempt to convert these companies. If their directors will not change by themselves, they will sooner or later be the objects of change. The people working in these companies who yearn for something else will quietly and calmly abandon them and either go to new companies or start their own.

The Capital Supply

Another technical issue that naturally emerges in this context is the capital supply of the new companies. Today, the capital supply, to a larger extent, is furnished in exchange for ownership and for monetary return on the capital invested. Essentially, this is done via stock exchanges. With the implementation of the ownership model suggested, the basis for this form of capital supply will dissipate. How, then, will the new companies be able to attract new capital when it is needed?

Although I cannot see anything specifically, I believe that the conditions are favorable for something to emerge. I believe this to be true because the ongoing development emanates from the change in human consciousness. This change and subsequent new way of thinking could be compared to that famous pebble thrown into the water. The water rings become wider and wider and encompass more and more aspects of our existence, eventually including our way of looking at capital and its use.

Even now, many individuals with surplus capital are looking for ways to invest outside the "normal" system. These individuals wish to avoid perpetuating business activities that do not correspond with their consciousness (such as the defense industry or operations that harm the environment). This desire for responsible investment has led to the birth of special stock funds that guarantee investors their capital will be used in ways harmonious with their values. I am aware of at least one such fund in Sweden. In the U.S. I know of four or five of considerable size.

In pace with the rise in consciousness, we will see many ways for the new companies to attract necessary capital. It is reasonable to assume that one such way will be mutual funds that exist primarily to give "energy" to the new enterprises. Such funds will be primarily interested in development rather than in ownership and return on investment.

CHAPTER 15

About the World Economy

- Work with personal and human development as its primary purpose.
- Businesses with the primary purpose of serving human development.
- Companies serving the market instead of exploiting it.
- Companies without any hierarchy or concentrations of power.
- Companies that do not strive to amass wealth and build economic value, but instead use their excess means to give energy to the process of their employees' personal development.
- Companies owned solely by the employees.
- A business life that is no longer production oriented, but, instead, focuses on giving nourishment to life.
- A business life that does not draw, drain or consume, but that nourishes, enriches and augments.

*I*s any of this at all feasible without a precipitating breakdown of our present economic system, without a collapse of the world economy?

I would like to answer that question in the following way: The end result of the present development will be a total change of the world economic picture. However, this change does not necessarily entail anything as dramatic as a collapse of the world economy. The new thought grows of its own force and does not require the ruins of the old one to serve as its fertile ground. A new economy could very well emerge as larger and larger islands within the old one before finally, without combat, taking over.

The World Economy Ultimately Rests on Air

However, the real question is whether the world economy has already collapsed. In any case, isn't our situation one of trying, with increasing difficulty, to hold up a system that has lost its vitality and has broken or is about to break down?

There are many indications that this is true. It is perhaps most evident when we look at the relations between the industrially developed world and the Third World.

According to a report published in July 1989 (only minor changes have occurred since then), the Third World's total burden of debt was the equivalent of U.S. $1.25 trillion. A portion of this debt is owed to such institutions as the International Monetary Fund and the World Bank. However, the largest portion of this debt, more than half, is owed to commercial banks in the industrialized world. The loans are commercial in that they carry interest. To serve this burden of debt, the developing countries are forced to ruthlessly exploit their natural as well as human resources.

Despite this exploitation, it will be impossible for the developing countries ever to honor their debts. Often they cannot even pay the interest. As we all know, the banks have solved this problem by simply rolling over the credits into new loans to which the interest is added. The developing countries, not having the money they need to service the loan, have to pay interest equivalent to approximately U.S. $25 million per day to industrialized countries that have more money than they need. This is exploitation of a degree that far surpasses that which took place during the time of so-called Colonialism.

To some extent, lenders have begun to accept that these debts will never be repaid. To mitigate the consequences of outright default, lenders have, among other things, forgiven parts of the debt amounts or depreciated the asset value of these loans on their balance sheets. However, the amounts involved in this respect are only drops in the ocean and are soon eaten up by the unpaid interest. The right thing to do would be to write off these loans fully and accept the consequences. That, however, cannot be done. These loans represent such a large part of the total balance sheets of so many banks that full write-offs would result in a breakdown of the industrialized world's banking system and, as a consequence, a breakdown of the world economy. Accordingly, banks and lending institutions continue to list these loans on balance sheets as assets, assets that in many cases are just so much air.

Is it too much to argue that the world economy is resting on air, that it is without substance? I do not think so. I think that most of us know of, or, in any case, have a feeling for these facts but choose to ignore them. We want to keep the illusion that "all is well—in our part of the world, anyway."

The System Cannot Bear Even Small Shocks

However, we need not go outside our part of the world to see how thin is the thread by which our system hangs. The world economy is based on development in the industrialized world, and this, in turn, is based on the vicious circle (production/consumption, increased production/increased consumption) we call economic growth. All hinges on two assumptions: that increased growth is, in reality, a possibility and that we as individuals are able and inclined to increase our consumption.

As concerns the factual possibility of yet more growth, suffice it to say that continued economic growth requires such a large depletion of our resources that the question of the survival of the economy must yield to the question of the survival of our planet. (When we talk about growth, we tend to forget that annual growth is built upon ever larger volume. Thus, a growth figure of 2.5 percent today represents four times the volume of a 2.5 percent growth rate during the 1950s. Projected over a long period, grotesque figures result: an economic growth rate of 2.5 to 3 percent compounded annually would in less than one hundred years increase our standard of living about twenty times. We could have twenty cars instead of one, for instance. In two hundred years our standard of living would increase about four hundred times.)

In contrast to the apparatuses (be they states, large corporations or financial institutions), individual human beings are now beginning to understand the problem with growth. Large numbers of people are also beginning to resent being held captive by the economic system. They are aware that increased consumption—their consumption—is the only possible way to sustain the present system. If people, out of pure instinct for self-preservation, started to consume less instead of increasing their consumption, the system would collapse.

As far as I can understand, no large, organized change in consumer patterns is needed to cause such a collapse. The system has become so fragile that it cannot withstand even small shocks.

This is a consequence of the economies within the industrialized world also having become debt economies.

Not only do most industrialized countries have debts—in many cases enormous debts—but corporations also have enormous debts. Investigations in Germany as well as in the United States show that, on average, forty to fifty percent of a product's selling price is used to cover the capital costs of the producer(s). In fact, seventy-one percent of the 1989 earnings of U.S. companies went to interest payments. In addition to governments and businesses, the majority of individual citizens in industrialized countries also have large and growing burdens of personal debt. For example, the total outstanding balance on U.S. credit cards, at the end of 1980, amounted to almost $55 billion; by the end of 1989, it had increased to almost $175 billion.

This debt economy requires growth for its existence. If the economic wheels do not spin—and they won't without growth, which is to say, increased consumption—banks and other lenders will not get the amortization and interest necessary for their continued existence. Without a functioning banking and finance system, our economic system cannot function.

We have put ourselves in a totally untenable position and have created a thorough mess in our efforts to support a system that is worn out and finished. Not only that, there is unabated competition for further growth. To express it another way: For companies to sell their goods (and if they cannot, the system will not work), consumers must have incomes big enough to service the debts of their nation and state (by paying taxes), their own debts (by paying amortization and interest) and, finally, corporate debts (by paying prices for goods and services that adequately cover the companies' costs of capital). Thus, ultimately, it all hinges on the individual: his or her ability and, of course, his or her willingness to consume.

The world economic system is in an utterly fragile state. Before, it could endure a squall now and then. Now, it can hardly even bear a small puff of wind. This economy has no substance or support. Even minor changes, for instance of the consumption level, would cause the whole thing to break down.

Actually, nothing is needed, as was demonstrated on October 19, 1987. On that day, the value of all the world's public companies dropped between twenty and fifty percent (the average fall in value was somewhere in the area of twenty-five percent). And what had happened? Had twenty-five percent of the companies' buildings burned down? Had some natural catastrophe or some war suddenly cut off the companies from twenty-five percent of their markets? Had some economic superpower made a drastic depreciation or appreciation of its currency? Had the consumer purchasing power suffered a sudden, radical decline? No, nothing had happened.

Two years later, by fall 1989, the companies' values were back to, if not greater than previous levels. What changes had occurred in the meantime? Had the companies found gold or diamonds? No, nothing had happened.

Is it an overstatement, then, to say that the economy rests on air, that it is without substance?

We can go on and examine the system of currencies that is an important part of the world's economic house of cards. The relative values of national currencies are decisively important to the stability of the world economy. Nonetheless, they are only fictitious figures lacking any real substance. Currency values seem to be picked out of the air. The arbitrariness becomes very evident when a particular exchange rate, not behaving according to the rules, either rises or drops in a way considered to be adventurous. To counteract this deviation, several central banks take action, by supporting purchases or sales, and manipulate the rate to bring it back to its "right" course.

The illusionary quality of this aspect of the economy becomes even more evident when a country, acting alone and with no warning, suddenly reevaluates its currency. In 1982 the then newly elected social democratic government of Sweden, in its first days in power, suddenly depreciated the Swedish Krona by sixteen percent. By no means did that mean that the substance of the Swedish economy had suddenly dropped by sixteen percent. It did mean, however, that Swedish products became more competitive on the world market. This competitive edge was not because Swedish products became better, more durable or more sophisticated. Nor was the cost of production decreased. Swedish products became more competitive on international markets because of currency manipulation. Such manipulations occur in spite of all international agreements and conventions designed to prevent them. That they occur at all demonstrates the inherent weakness of this cornerstone upon which world economy rests.

Speculation, the Real Cancerous Tumor

The lack of substance in our economy has opened the gates for one of the real cancerous tumors of the system, the one of speculation. Both individuals and institutions, having made or borrowed more money than they need, are choosing not to invest this excess capital in actual development. Instead, they are investing in positive or negative expectations about money itself; they are speculating in currencies, bonds, stocks, convertibles and, in recent times, in futures and options (these seem created directly for speculative purposes).

There is speculation in real estate, commodities and art. (The latest gimmick is to buy shares in a work of art that is then put into some bank vault to "grow"—hardly what the artist intended for the work.) Banks, insurance companies and other highly respected institutions are deeply engaged in speculative activities, both directly through their speculating, and indirectly by speculating for clients or consulting in the business of speculation. If an institution is powerful enough, or if a group of institutions can somehow discretely coordinate its efforts, it can even direct the development in ways which are beneficial to itself and its clients.

The speculative portion of our economy is larger by volume than any other part. Estimations made by the U.S. Department of Commerce show that in 1989 (and only marginal changes have occurred since then) the total value of world trade amounted to U.S. $2.8 trillion. The total world financial flows, however, that same year amounted to more than U.S. $80 trillion. Speculators are called actors in the money and capital market and consist of individuals (called financiers), small companies, large companies, communities, funds and so on. What they have in common is that they try to make money out of money. They do not augment anything and don't even try to do so. They take and grab. The speculative economy consists of nothing but continual transfers of money from one hand to another. Money, originally a means of facilitating commerce, a medium of exchange, has now become a commodity in and of itself. An activity in essence consisting of nothing more than buying and selling money does not contribute anything of substance to the economy. On the contrary, it drains power and energy from the economy until the economy is finally devoured. More importantly, such an activity makes no contribution to individual human beings.

Speculative activities—the largest part of our economy—have lives apart from the human sphere. Nevertheless, their existence is dependent upon us as individuals. Why? If people do not maintain and preferably increase their levels of consumption, companies cannot dispose of their products. If companies cannot dispose of their products, they cannot distribute to the employees the income needed not only for buying the products per se but also for paying the debt costs of the government, their own debt costs, the debt costs of the companies and so on. The spiral continues its inexorable turn, and there will soon be nothing in which to speculate.

The Interest Rate System, Yet Another Cancerous Tumor

I do not think it is particularly difficult to see that speculation is one of the true cancerous tumors on the world economy, sometimes referred to as a casino-economy. These speculative activities are often attacked, but without any results, it seems.

There is, however, another particularly virulent tumor that is rarely attacked or even questioned. It is the fundamental part of our economic system that says money can generate money: the interest rate system. Not only is money bought and sold, but also the very use of money is bought and sold.

I have often wondered why one of the world's great religions, the Muslim faith, so expressly bans the charging of interest. (The fact that ways have been found in modern times to bypass this ban is not relevant in this context.) In all likelihood, this prohibition is not a whim. There must be a higher thought behind it. There also must have been a higher thought behind the fact that in other great religions, such as Christianity and Judaism in their original forms, charging interest was banned, at least within their respective groups.

Perhaps the prohibition against the charging of interest grew from notions that all human beings are alike, that we all have the same rights and no one has the right to exercise power over anyone else. That one who happens to have more money than he or she needs should be able to increase that wealth by selling the use of the surplus to one who has less money than he or she needs is in direct conflict with this higher thought. It encourages inequality, injustice and the growth of power structures.

Perhaps only now we can see how devastating this system is. Perhaps only now we can see the wisdom behind the admonitions of such great thinkers as Moses, Buddha, Jesus and Mohammed. Paradoxically, it is probably precisely the debt-ridden and speculative economy we have to thank for our growing clear-sightedness. These economic conditions both clarify and magnify the effects of the interest rate system. This, combined with a long period (in the U.S. with a temporary break in the election year of 1992) with high interest rate levels, has started a new spiral to unfold. In spite of many political efforts, we have not been able to slow it down or stop it. In this spiral, money is being transferred at an ever-accelerating rate from those having less than they need to those who have more than they need.

To comprehend this scope, we must keep in mind that we pay interest—capital costs—not only when we borrow money but also each time we purchase a product, pay our rent, or make any similar transaction. As mentioned previously, the capital-cost portion of a price, on average, is about fifty percent. So, some fifty percent of what we in the industrialized countries spend on necessities—on food, clothes, durable goods and housing—is, in reality, interest costs.

Within this scenario, only a small part of the population has more income from interest than what is paid in interest costs. (Look at your own finances: Even if you have no loans and maybe some money in the bank, you would probably find that expenses for interest exceed income from interest.) In these circumstances, we can clearly see the process that is accelerating the polarization between the poor and the wealthy. Although I haven't seen the precise figures, I believe it to be an accurate estimation that the portion of the population in industrialized countries who benefit from the interest system (whose income from interest exceeds the expenses for interest) is about ten percent.

To summarize, we see that developing countries, with ninety percent of the world's population, are paying enormous sums of interest to industrialized countries, with only ten percent of the world's population. Within these industrialized countries, positive capital flow is concentrated within a group of people representing some ten percent of the population. Thus, one percent (ten percent of ten percent) of the world's population is multiplying its riches at the expense of the remaining ninety-nine percent!

It is inevitable that this spiral leads to a concentration of wealth. It is also inevitable that this concentration will increase and accelerate. We can see examples of this all over the world, especially within the industrial sector. Small- and mid-size companies are being purchased by large companies. The large companies are being purchased by even larger companies that, in turn, are being purchased by giants. In 1988 the equivalent of U.S. $70 billion was spent in Europe on buy-outs. And now the giants have begun buying out each other. Practically every week there are announcements of one big merger after another. (One striking example is the merger, announced in August 1989, between two

Big Eight auditing giants, resulting in an auditing firm with more than seventy thousand employees!)

To some extent, these buy-outs are the results of giant companies seeking a large-scale advantage. More often, though, it is the result of a relatively small number of companies seeking ways of investing excess means. This development has progressed to the point that many large corporations can now make more money on financial operations than on the production of goods. Production has become a facade for banking. It is not inconceivable that this trend will eventually result in all the world's industry being controlled by some twenty-five or so giant corporations powerful enough to make the marionette roles of governments and international organizations only too evident. At that point, if not before, the economic house of cards will collapse with a crash, partly due to its own weight and partly due to people's unwillingness (being wiser than the apparatuses) to participate in such an inequitable system.

Is a System Without Interest Possible?

Can an economic system exist without interest? Yes, of course it can, as long as there is some impetus to keep money in circulation. After the interest system is abolished, many solutions to this question will emerge. In a brilliant book by Magrit Kennedy, (*Interest Free and Inflation Free Money,* Permakultur Institute, v., Ginsterweg 4-5, D-3074 Steyerberg, Germany. Original English text.), one such solution is suggested: replace interest rates with a nominal fee on money that is not in circulation. Such a fee would apply to all money, including the cash balances of the banks.

However, I do not think that a system without interest rates would necessarily need any technical incentives to keep money in circulation. The concept of wholeness, so characteristic of the new way of thinking, will redirect our focus on what is beneficial from the self to a more encompassing view. Any excess means will be managed under principles that benefit the whole of society. In the new thought, we will know that if it is a detriment to society that our excess money is not in circulation, then it is also a detriment to ourselves. Or stated in the reverse, if it is of benefit to the whole that excess money is kept in circulation, then it also is of benefit to the individual.

To Sum Up

Our economic system is based on growth resulting from ever-increasing consumption. We humans, being wiser than the apparatuses that rule our economies, are becoming more and more aware that we are captives of these economic systems, systems that have brought our civilization and our planet to the edge of catastrophe. We are, therefore, becoming disposed to consume less, not more. The world economy is without substance; its structural fragility, created by speculation, indebtedness and a long period of high interest rates, cannot withstand any shocks, large or small (decreased consumption, for instance). The flow of money from poor countries to rich countries and from poor people to the giant fortunes of the "capital collectors" in the developed countries have brought to light the basic injustices inherent in the existing economic system. Here lies a self-timed bomb ticking; the more evident the injustices become, the closer the detonation.

And finally, the entire system rests on so much air: assets in the form of loans from the industrialized countries to the Third World. Isn't this the greatest illusion ever?

It is difficult to believe that this system can survive much longer.

Besides, what will happen when the Third World finally calls for its rights on our planet?

CHAPTER *16*

On Our Way

*W*e are evolving; we are on our way. Human consciousness is rising. Although it may not yet be obvious, we are at the beginning of a radical and dramatic change in the human condition. By the beginning of the next century, we will be able to look back on the intervening period as the greatest revolution ever. It is not a revolution fought with blood or weapons. It is a revolution of thought; it is a revolution born out of our longing.

All aspects of life are affected by this revolution. It erases the borders separating the countries of the earth. It eliminates the inequitable distribution of wealth. It recognizes the uniqueness as well as the equality of all human beings. It re-creates a unity of nature and humanity.

A new economy is emerging. Perhaps it will have characteristics similar to those I have described in this book; perhaps somewhat different. Whatever the specific characteristics may be, this new economy will serve humanity and nature, not draw, drain and consume. This economy will bring people together, not separate them.

We see how companies that reflect the new thought emerge as islands in the sea of the old economy. Some have been mentioned in this book, and there are many more.

One of the early pioneers is W.L. Gore & Associates, Inc. (Gore), headquartered in Newark, Delaware (mentioned in Chapter 9, "About Organization"). Gore has been practicing a very nontraditional management and organizational structure—The Lattice System—for more than thirty years. This family-held plastics company started in 1958 in the basement of its founders' home, the late Bill Gore and his wife, Genevieve. Its main product is a synthetic fiber, Gore-Tex, used in fabrics and many medical, electronic and industrial products. To the public, Gore is probably best known for its breathable yet waterproof fabric used in camping and other outdoor equipment.

Bill Gore left a seventeen-year employment as a research chemist with Du Pont to start his company. He decided to keep away from the suffocating bureaucracies of the traditional companies, and the Lattice System—often referred to as a system of nonmanagement—was introduced. The basis of the system concerns human relations: instead of the fixed lines and levels of relations within the typical hierarchy, the Lattice organization provides for and urges direct person-to-person transactions and self-commitment.

The company philosophy is based on four principles Bill Gore outlined in a company memorandum:

Fairness

It is necessary for all of us to try to be fair in order to maintain and preserve the good feelings among us. Deliberate or thoughtless unfairness generates resentment and anger, destroying the cooperation and communication required for good teamwork.

Freedom

Freedom is the source of inventions, innovations, and creativity. Trying new ideas involves risk as well as requiring effort, thought, and imagination. The risk factor can lead to mistakes. All of us need the freedom to make mistakes.

Commitment

Consistency of principles require projects and functions by free commitment rather than by systems of authoritarian command . . .

Waterline

Security and success of the Enterprise require that we be discreet in the exercise of our freedom if the reputation, financial security, or future opportunities of the Enterprise are at risk. Consultation with appropriate associates is necessary before actions taken that may involve these risks.

[In company parlance, such "risky" actions are often referred to as "drilling holes under the waterline"].

As a consequence, at Gore there are no titles (except sometimes for legal, external purposes). There are no executive parking lots. Nor are there any big, impressive executive offices. There is no chain of command. There are no "employees." Each individual worker is an associate. There are no bosses. Plant and staff department teams are headed by leaders. The leaders have little, if any (external) power or authority. They cannot give orders and may only seek (not require) commitments from associates. Commitment—the making and keeping of promises by self-motivated, self-directed and self-controlled associates—is the very backbone of the company. The leaders cannot hire or fire associates without consent from peer committees and the "sponsor" assigned to the individual in question. Sponsors replace traditional companies' supervisors. A sponsor (each associate has one) is not there to control. He or she is the associate's guide, a mentor functioning as a counsel and advocate.

Not surprising, the work environment within this company is one of personal fulfillment, creativity and innovation, resulting in business success. Since its start in 1958, Gore has experienced an almost explosive development. What started out as a basement shop now meets all criteria for a Fortune 500 company. As of spring 1992, Gore employs some 5,300 associates in forty-six plants (as discussed in Chapter 9, the number of plants increases because the company starts new plants when any plant reaches a size of 150-200 associates) throughout the world, in the U.S., France, Germany, Japan and Scotland. Annual sales exceed $700 million and, when it comes to return on assets and equity, Gore ranks in the top five percent of major U.S. companies.

You may wonder, Is the success of Gore really attributable to its system of "un-management"? Isn't it, rather, attributable to the fact that the company has the good fortune of having extraordinary and absolutely unique products? If you ask these questions of any Gore associate, you will get this straight answer: "This company is built on innovation. Our unique products are results of this innovation, which, in its turn, is the result of the Lattice System."

We see these island companies, which reflect the new way of thinking, emerging in the sea of the old economy in the U.S., with its distinctive traditions. We see them emerging in Scandinavia, with its distinctive traditions. And we see them in other parts of the world with even more different traditions, as in Brazil, for instance.

One example is Promon Tecnologia S.A., founded in 1970 and located in Sao Paulo, Brazil. Promon S.A. is a consulting company active in the fields of technical construction and architecture. It employs about four thousand people, all of whom have the exclusive right to own shares of the company. No one, though, can own more than five percent of the share capital. The board as well as the executive management is elected by the employees (share-holders) for three years. Promon's charter expressly prescribes that the main aims of the company are to serve its customers and to serve the personal and professional development of its employees.

The company is profitable. Yet the charter prescribes that profit is not one of its basic objectives, even if profit constitutes an "indispensable prerequisite for the stability and development of the company. It is rather a means for the achievement of its ends."

In a letter to me (published in the August 1989 issue of *Perspectives*, a monthly publication of the World Business Academy, Burlingame, California), Tamas Makray, one of Promon's founders and the current chairman, explained some of the basic principles of the company:

> It is terrible to be an employee and depend totally on the owners of the business. . . . The staff spends most of the day at the work place, may spend their entire professional lives in the company with colleagues and friends, so what happens there is very important to them—often more important to them than to the owners.
>
> Privileges are so ugly. We should try to be equal. Ideally all employees should be more or less equal shareholders and participate in at least those decisions that affect them directly.
>
> Conflict between capital and labor (owners and staff) is mortal. It goes against the very nature of any adventure that is based on cooperation, or even better, co-creation, by all stakeholders.

Another Brazilian example is Semco A/S (see Chapter 9, "About Organization"). In his intriguing article, "Managing Without Managers" (*Harvard Business Review* September-October 1989), Semco's president, Ricardo Semler, tells the story of Semco's turnaround.

When Semler joined the company in 1980, Semco was a sleepy, one-hundred-employee manufacturer of hydraulic pumps, generating some U.S. $4 million in revenues and at the edge of financial catastrophe. By 1988, Semco had established itself as one of the fastest growing companies of Brazil with a profit margin of ten percent on sales of U.S. $37 million generated by some eight hundred employees (also here called associates) and repeatedly named as the best company to work for in Brazil. And all this growth was bank financed at interest rates generally thirty percent above the rate of inflation, which ranged from forty percent to nine hundred percent annually!

How was this possible? Semler mentioned hard work and good luck. "But most important I think were the drastic changes we made in our concept of management."

Semco's company philosophy rests on three basic values: democracy (the employees can overrule—and have done so—crucial management decisions), profit sharing (twenty-three percent of after-tax profit is distributed to the workers) and information (each employee has total access to all critical information, the executive payroll included).

Semco has replaced the organizational pyramid of the traditional company by three concentric circles: one small, central circle of five people (called counselors) who integrate the operations of the company, a second circle containing eight division heads (called partners) and a third circle containing all other employees. Among those in the third circle are some permanent or temporary team and task leaders. These are called coordinators. Thus, there are four titles and three management layers. Wrote Semler,

> The linchpins in the system are the coordinators, a group including everyone formerly called foreman, supervisor, manager, head, or chief. The only people who report to coordinators are

associates. No coordinator reports to another coordinator. . . .
That feature of the system is what ensures the reduction in
management layers.

With Semco there are no dress codes. There are no time clocks
(workers—even on the factory floor—set their own working sched-
ules). Nor are there any company rules about travel expenses
(those are replaced by each individual's common sense). In essence—and here I think the real source of Semco's survival is to
be found—Semco, as Semler put it, hires "adults, and then we treat
them as adults."

> Think about that. Outside the factory, workers are men and
> women who elect governments, serve in the army, lead com-
> munity projects, raise and educate families, and make decisions
> every day about the future. Friends solicit their advice. Sales-
> people court them. Children and grandchildren look up to them
> for their wisdom and experience. But the moment they walk
> into the factory, the company transforms them into adolescents.
> They have to bear badges and name tags, arrive at a certain
> time, stand in line to punch the clock or eat their lunch, get
> permission to go to the bathroom, give lengthy explanations
> every time they're five minutes late, and follow instructions
> without asking a lot of questions.

Semco has replaced "all the nitpicking regulations with the
rule of common sense," putting its employees in the "demanding
position of using their own judgment."

Yes, I want to think about that! I want to think about how we
can bring life into our workplaces, can create living companies
by replacing mistrust with trust, by entrusting instead of super-
vising and commanding. What stops us? What stops us other than
our fear—our own mistrust in ourselves?

We also see examples of alternative economic systems emerging or rather completing the old economic systems. The most interesting one I am aware of is to be found in several communities in so-called depressed areas in Canada. This system is called The Local Exchange Trading System (LET).

The departure point for LET is a local economy that has become paralyzed and is suffering from high unemployment and the resultant psychosocial problems, problems that demand costly efforts and contributions from the larger society. According to the founders of LET, this state of affairs is not necessarily due to the lack of trade in these areas. More often, it is argued, these problems are the result of the centralization of the national economy.

The surplus generated by the economic activity in one geographical area is taken away to a remote company headquarters, in some cases located in another part of the world. The means of conducting economic activity—the money—leaves the area where it was generated. This condition is often compounded by restrictions on the money supply, restrictions imposed by the central government in its efforts to improve the national economy, sometimes at the expense of local economies.

Economic depression, the paralyzing of local economies, is then, in reality, an artificially created condition. The depression is not the result of trade or activity not being needed, but rather of a scarcity of means with which to conduct the trade.

To neutralize this condition, LET has created a new currency, unique to each respective community. This currency is often called green dollars in contrast to the "real" Canadian dollar.

The heart of LET is a microcomputer that functions as a community bulletin board. With this bulletin board, the inhabitants of the community, by telephone, mail or personal visits, can advertise the goods and services they need or want to sell. The bulletin board has a built-in accounting system that works like an ordinary bank account. The money that is accounted for, however, is not Canadian dollars but electronic green dollars.

The account of each participating community member starts at zero. Then, when a transaction takes place (Person A paints Person B's house, Person C sells firewood, a car or whatever to Person D), it is registered in the accounting system by acknowledging receipt of the goods or service. The purveyor's account is credited with an amount of green dollars agreed upon by the parties. These dollars—sometimes in combination with real dollars—can then be used to acquire some needed goods or services advertised on the bulletin board.

The system allows credit, and members can make overdrafts. The credit is extended without interest or overdraft costs. The seller, therefore, can always be sure of getting paid. Unlike the cash-based system, a shortage of money does not halt trade; when a transaction is completed, the seller can immediately circulate green points within the system.

LET is now in operation in some twenty communities in Canada as well as some in Australia, New Zealand, England and Wales. In communities where the system has had time to become established, the local economies have recovered to a marked degree. This recovery has been experienced by individuals, families and businesses alike. Business can sell goods and services for partial payment in green dollars without adversely affecting the cash flow. Lack of cash, then, does not impede any needed growth.

Another important benefit is that people who use LET feel better about themselves and have come closer to others within their communities.

So it is possible, even now, to create economic systems based on cooperation and concern for human beings instead of systems way above our heads, instead of abstractions that enslave us human beings. The only limitations to innovations in this direction are the ones we ourselves establish.

In this context I cannot keep from reflecting on what at the time of this writing (winter 1992) is going on in the Eastern bloc and, especially, in the former Soviet Union. The Soviets are in the enviable position of having faced complete economic collapse. This is enviable because there is no longer anything to defend; a new system can be constructed without the restrictions imposed by attitudes of prestige and defensiveness. Perhaps by intensely scrutinizing the West's economic system—and even trying it— they will see the cavities, the inhumanity and the devastating effects this economic model is having on our planet. Perhaps the Eastern bloc eventually will try to avoid replacing political captivity with the economic captivity that is unavoidable in the Western economic system. Perhaps something new will emerge out of the economic chaos in that part of the world. Perhaps a new, human economy will be established and will become the example we all will eventually follow.

Finally

Regardless of where and under what circumstances the new economic forms emerge, economic issues will not be of paramount importance in future societies. The purpose of societies will no longer have an economic signature. The basic purpose of societies will be the enabling of their members to develop the highest possible degree of personal potential.

The central institutions of these societies will not be the economic power centers of the societies of today. These central institutions will not be confederations of businesses or trade unions, nor banks or large corporations. Rather, the central institutions will be knowledge centers of different kinds. Perhaps they will be universities or academies. We are not, as is sometimes argued, becoming information societies; we are becoming learning societies. This learning, however, is not something to be pursued only at certain times in only certain places. This learning is a process; it is life itself in all its aspects. Is it too utopian to go so far as to suggest that the final vision is the wisdom society?

In any case, we are on our way.

CHAPTER *17*

At Last

*Y*ou!

When you go out in nature next time, perhaps to wander
in the forests,
Then, sit down on a rock in the meadow.
Watch the sun find its way through the foliage and, with its
warmth and its light caressing the tree trunks, the moss on
the ground, the rock you are sitting upon,
Feel it caressing you.
Hear the birds sing out their joy of life.
Look down at the ground and rejoice at all the thousands
of small, creeping things at your feet.
Quiet yourself for a while
And you will sense the total harmony of the tree, the flower,
the buzzards hovering high above you.
Sense the total harmony contained within each one,
Sense the total harmony between each and the other,
Sense the total harmony between all the elements of nature.
Here there is no fear,
No striving for power.
No worries about tomorrow,
Here is no past,

Here is no future.

Only one single now.

You are a part of all this.

If you listen carefully, you can hear nature

telling you that you belong,

that there are no distances.

If you stay a while in stillness,

you also can hear the weeping.

It is the weeping of a mother who cannot understand why

the children she gave birth to

are devouring her, poisoning her, draining her life-juice

and do not seem to care that she is dying.

Her despair is deep.

But, between the tears, as you rest in bountiful stillness, you can also

feel a hopeful smile coming forward

and also as someone trying to whisper to you.

After a while you can distinguish the words.

They are saying:

The humans are on their way back. The humans at last give in to

their longing, their longing home!

RECOMMENDED READING

Books

Catford, L. and Ray, M. *The Path of the Everyday Hero.* Los Angeles: Jeremy P. Tarcher 1991.

Harman, W. *Global Mind Change:* The Promise of the Last Years of the Twentieth Century. New York: Warner Books 1990.

Harman, W. and Horman, J. *Creative Work: The Constructive Role of Business in a Transforming Society.* Indianapolis: Knowledge Systems, Inc., 1990.

Land, G. and Jarman, B. *Breakpoint and Beyond: Mastering the Future—Today.* New York: Harper Collins 1992.

Orsborn, C. *Inner Excellence: Spiritual Principles of Life-Driven Business.* San Rafael, California: New World Library 1992.

Ray, M. and Myers, R. *Creativity in Business.* New York: Doubleday 1989.

Ray, M. and Rintzler, A. Ed. *The New Paradigm in Business: Emerging Strategies for Leadership and Organizational Change.* Los Angeles: Jeremy P. Tarcher 1993.

Periodicals

Perspectives. Quarterly Journal, published by the World Business Academy, Burlingame, California.

The New Leaders, Newsletter, published by Sterling & Stone, Berkeley, California.

At Work: Stories of Tomorrow's Workplace, Newsletter, published by Berret-Koeler, San Francisco, California.

ABOUT THE AUTHOR

Rolf Österberg, founding member of The World Business Academy, is a seasoned executive in the film and newspaper industries. He has served as president and CEO of Svensk Filmindustri, Scandinavia's largest film company; president, CEO and Chairman of the Board of the Swedish Newspapers association; and executive vice president and deputy CEO of the Dagens Nyheter Group, Sweden's largest newspaper group. He was also chairman of the board of over twenty companies and trade associations. He has a law degree from the University of Stockholm, Sweden. He has also attended the senior management program of the Harvard Business School. *Corporate Renaissance*, his first book, was originally published in Sweden, where it was a bestseller.

Österberg lectures and gives seminars around the world on the relationship between humans and the business organization in a changing society. He lives in Stockholm, Sweden and Stinson Beach, California.

For information on lectures or seminars by the author, please write or fax:

Rolf Österberg
P.O. Box 994
Stinson Beach, CA 94970
Fax: 415-868-2362

OR

During summer months:

Rolf Österberg
Vastmannagatan 30
11325 Stolkholm, Sweden
Fax: Int. + 46-8-149888

A NOTE ON THE TYPE

This book was set in Zapf Book Light and Demibold, with Fenice Regular and Bold used as display.

OTHER BOOKS AND TAPES
FROM NATARAJ PUBLISHING

Books

Living in the Light: A Guide to Personal and Planetary Transformation. By Shakti Gawain with Laurel King. The recognized classic on developing intuition and using it as a guide in living your life. (Trade paperback $9.95)

Living in the Light Workbook. By Shakti Gawain. Following up her bestseller, *Living in the Light,* Shakti has created a workbook to help us apply these principles to our lives in very practical ways. (Trade paperback $12.95)

Return to the Garden: A Journey of Discovery. By Shakti Gawain. Shakti reveals her path to self-discovery and personal power and shows us how to return to our personal garden and live on earth in a natural and balanced way. (Trade paperback $9.95)

Awakening: A Daily Guide to Conscious Living. By Shakti Gawain. A daily meditation guide that focuses on maintaining your spiritual center not just when you are in solitude, but when you are in the world, and especially, in relationships. (Trade paperback $8.95)

Embracing Our Selves: The Voice Dialogue Manual. By Drs. Hal and Sidra Stone. The highly acclaimed, groundbreaking work that explains the psychology of the selves and the Voice Dialogue method. (Trade paperback $12.95)

Embracing Each Other: Relationship as Teacher, Healer, and Guide. By Drs. Hal and Sidra Stone. A compassionate guide to understanding and improving our relationships. The follow-up to the Stone's pioneering book on Voice Dialogue. (Trade paperback $11.95)

Maps to Ecstasy: Teachings of an Urban Shaman. By Gabrielle Roth with John Loudon. A modern shaman shows us how to reconnect to the vital energetic core of our being, by showing us how dance, song, theater, writing, meditation, and ritual can awaken the healer in each of us. (Trade paperback $9.95)

Notes from My Inner Child: I'm Always Here. By Tanha Luvaas. This deeply touching book puts us directly in contact with the tremendous energy and creativity of the inner child. (Trade paperback $8.95)

Coming Home: The Return to True Self. By Martia Nelson. A down-to-earth spiritual primer that explains how we can use the very flaws of our humanness to carry the vibrant energy of our true self and reach the potential that dwells in all of us. (Trade paperback $12.95)

Corporate Renaissance: Business as an Adventure in Human Development. By Rolf Osterberg. This groundbreaking book explodes the myth that a business's greatest asset is capital, and shows why employees must come first for businesses to succeed in the 90s. (Hardcover $18.95)

Tapes

Living in the Light: Shakti Gawain Reads Her Bestseller. (Two cassettes $15.95)

Developing Intuition. Shakti Gawain expands on the ideas about intuition she first discussed in *Living in the Light*. (One cassette $10.95)

To Place an Order

Call 1-800-949-1091.

Nataraj Publishing is committed to acting as a catalyst for change and transformation in the world by providing books and tapes on the leading edge in the fields of personal and social consciousness growth. "Nataraj" is a Sanskrit word referring to the creative, transformative power of the universe. For more information on our company or to purchase our products, please contact us at:

Nataraj Publishing
P.O. Box 2627
Mill Valley, CA 94942
Phone: 415-381-1091
Fax: 415-381-1093